Forward by Jeffery Pritchett

I first met Shebaz Butt aka Beezlebub on Facebook while he was doing The Electric Eye Radio show. We conversed, and eventually, somehow he became one of my co-hosts for The Church of Mabus radio show. He probably answered one of my statuses. My memory is shot from the long years of life in North America. We did many great shows together with guests like Peter Levenda and countless others too numerous to list.

I remember one off of the top of my head. Our Halloween show with Victor T. Foia on his book Dracula Chronicles, Son of the Dragon. A Halloween show on Vlad the Impaler from a Transylvanian. Loved that one and countless others. There was much weird synergy over the years. We both told our encounter stories to each other countless times. We also discussed Occult knowledge and the metaphysical and paranormal. We were having a bromance and life was good.

His schedule changed with work and hasn't done the show in a while and plans to return sometime in the future for visitations. He is a brother and always welcome within the confines of the walls of The Church Of Mabus radio show. I was very excited that he was writing The Bizarre Compendium Volume 1. A chance to get into this cat's head space and roam around a while on the wide open road of the high strange.

I know his energy will crawl up inside you like a strange alien probe and change you from within via his written words. From topics of the paranormal, serial murder, and the creepy. The book is a perfect bleeding ground for him to do his work. This being, whose mother named him after the devil in his childhood. This Beezlebub creature who is an interstellar traveler who has now fashioned from his clawed fingertips this manifesto that will forever change our world!

They say the knowledge and information of books, exist in the astral realm, on some level, and will pull it forth through our bodies like some obscene channel to manifest into our present now. I have written many books myself over the years, and at the time it was funny because I didn't know I was doing it. I was doing written interviews with people for several websites and finally had so many it made like 5 books when all was said and done. When you get in that flow, sometimes it overtakes you like a mad possession. This rhythm has hit Beezle, and we will see much more in this vein of his knowledge assembled for public viewing. The Bizarre Anthology is a reason excitement. One more arrow piercing the wall of normalcy to bring the bastard down in pieces finally.

But now let us start this grand adventure through The Bizarre Compendium Volume 1. It will forever leave you changed and transmuted via Faustian pacts and metaphors. Fasten your straight jacket and put on your Viking helmet and get ready for one strange ride! It's going to get weird ma! It's going to get damned weird!

Eternally yours, Jeffery Pritchett

www.churchofmabusradio.com

A Bizarre Anthology

DEATH

THE PARANORMAL

THE RAMBLINGS OF A MAD SORCERER

Why do most people slow down and try to get a better look at a car crash? A part of me would like to think that we do this out of a sense of concern and compassion for our fellow human beings. A larger part of me knows that we slow down because we want to see death. Maybe now you could catch a glimpse of the truth of life. I have often wondered why we are ushered so slowly past the scene of a brutal accident. The drama unfolds before you. You see the frantic angry flashing, red, yellow, and blue lights. You hear the insane wailing and whirring sirens, creating high anxiety and an audio-visual sensory overload, casting chaos in all directions. Forced to drive outside of the lines, you try to reposition yourself so these screeching mechanical harbingers of disaster can squeeze by. The traffic slows to an insidious crawl. The rubbernecking ensues smartphones are brought out to capture something interesting to post to a favored social network. The police slowly wave you by while a greater drama unfolds behind the shields that are ushering you back to safety.

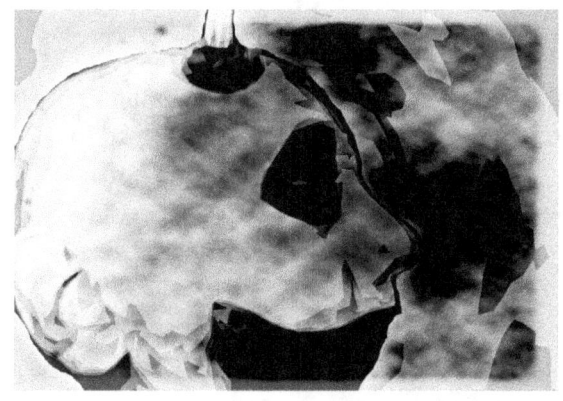

If you look past the distraction of a bottlenecked traffic control effort that is if you are still looking. The eye might spy emergency medical technicians frantically performing their healing craft attempting to stabilize the brutalized flesh and body of a rather unfortunate soul. Of course in turn we might see these same brave lifesavers dutifully tugging the resentful zipper of a body bag tight around a prone lifeless shape. A form you recognize all too clearly. Now in the same eye-full there may be firefighters rendering the steel and aluminum corpse of an overpriced luxury automobile asunder with the Jaws of Life. Who is to know? One thing that is for certain is that you had better reel your eyes back in from the depth of the scenario and get them back on the road to your destination.

The moment that you were a part of this grim reminder will potentially fade from your memory. The Memory will be lying sleeping and dormant in your subconscious until all of these moments create a jolly death parade. A parade marching behind your glazed over eyes in slow motion every time you are facing the prospect of the pale specter of the reaper! How are we to know?

On another hand this moment could define a person. After an experience like this someone might become inspired to save lives or even to take them. History shows that experience is subjective. Things tend to affect people in very different ways. An experience could lead you to seek answers to questions that may better be left unknown. Remember that once you go so far you can't go back and if you dig enough you will get to the bottom.

HP. Lovecraft Said, "The most merciful thing in the world, I think, is the inability of the human mind to correlate all its contents. We live on a placid island of ignorance in the midst of black seas of the infinity, and it was not meant that we should voyage far." - Lovecraft - (The Call of Cthulu)

I think he was right.

The book that you are holding in your hands is a small piece of a personal Necronomicon. A sheet flayed from the quivering skin of my subconscious mind. In your hands are the sounds of beetle wings and cricket legs scraping across each other in the darkness. This book is a car crash brutal, violent, and terrifying. Some of you might have a hard time putting it down. Some of you might set it down and never pick it up again. Most of you will have a hard time not taking a glance at it. The book, as it lurks there, in between the spines of your bookcase like a baleful eye. An eye that seems to see right through you every time you walk by. Do you dare linger? Do you dare crack this infernal tome open? For what is inside will scar your mind and take you away from what you know and what makes you feel safe. Enter at your own risk.

Pembly Tower West
Old Salem
1997

A
BIZARRE
COMPENDIUM

VOLUME 1

WRITTEN EDITED AND CREATED BY SHEBAZ BUTT

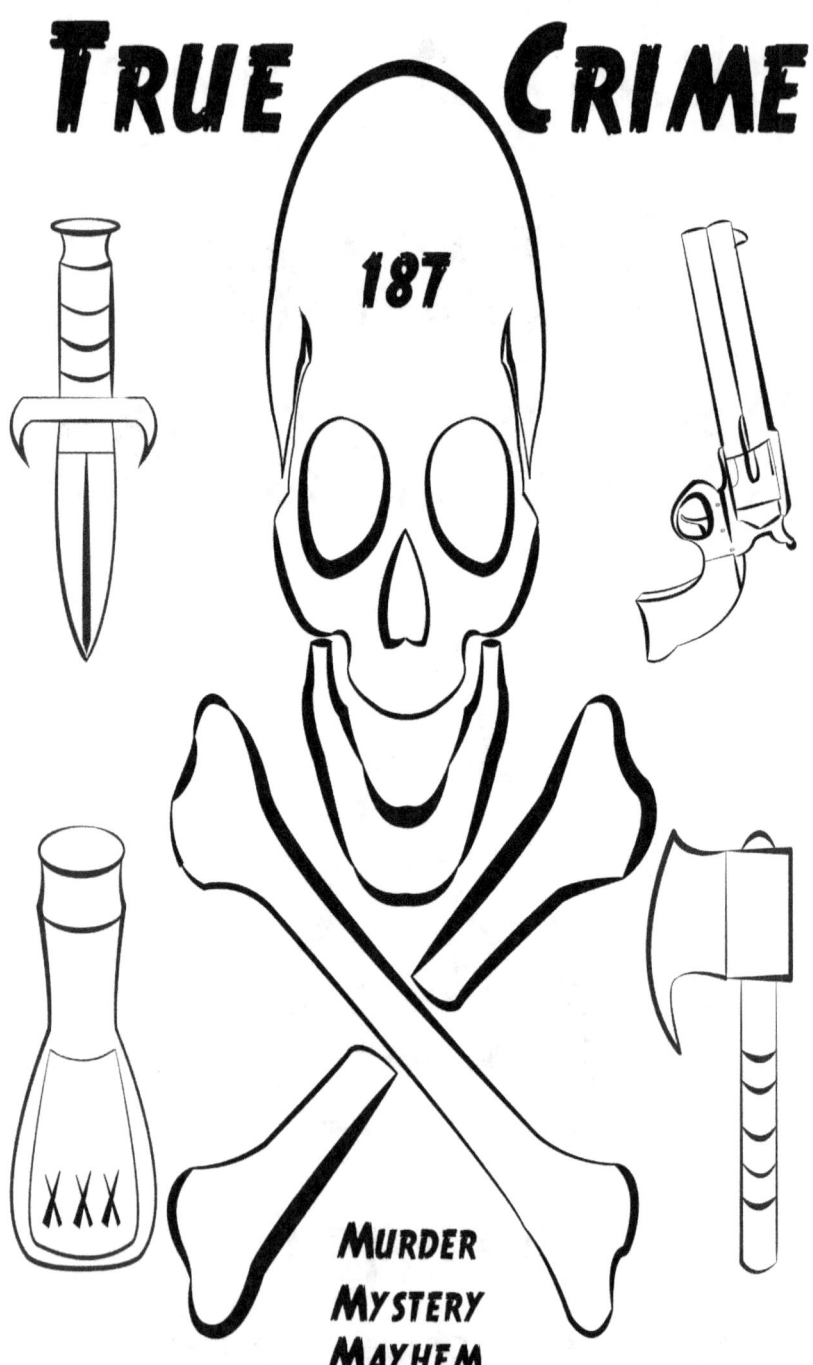

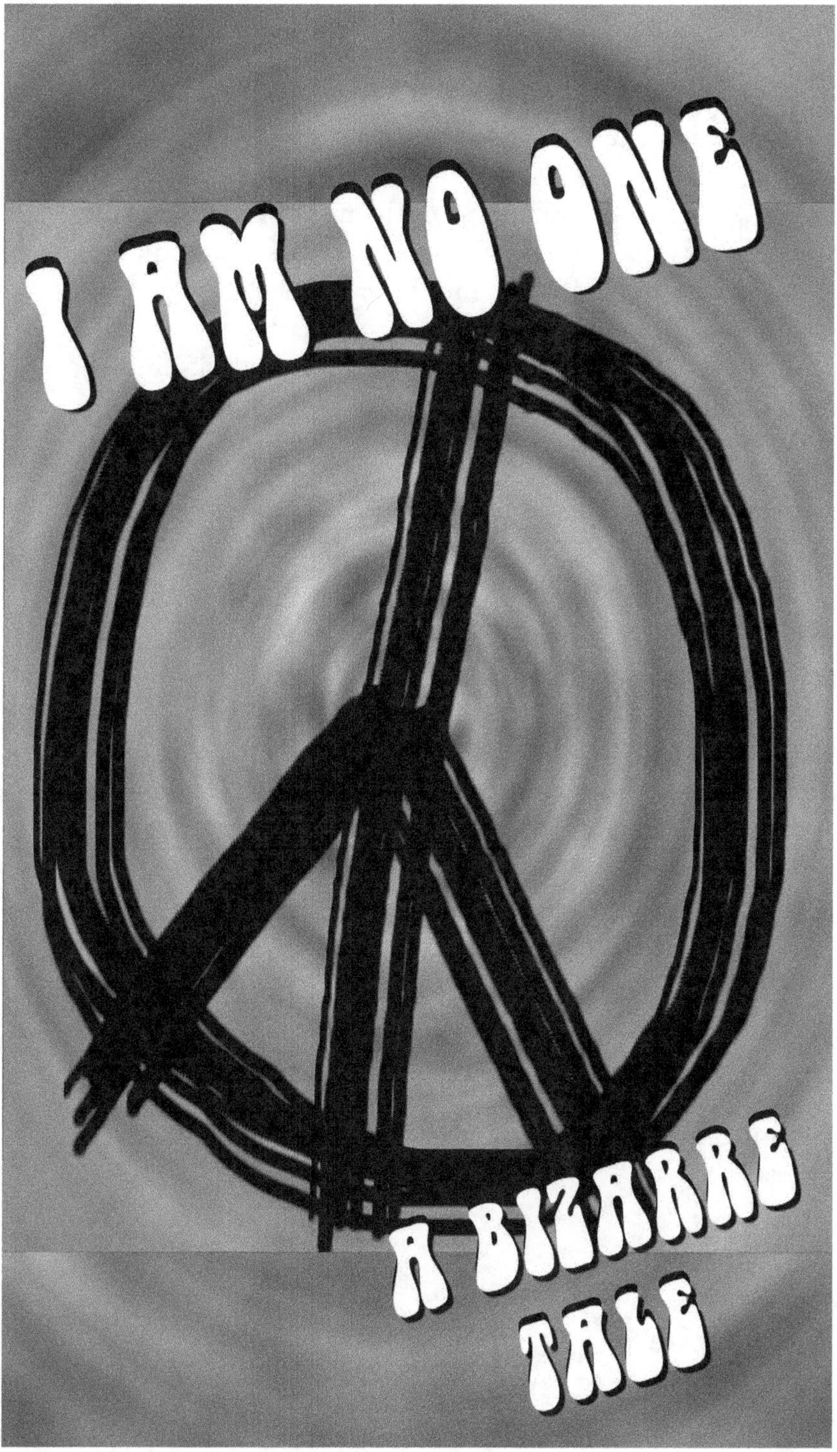
I AM NO ONE
A BIZARRE
TALE

Helter Skelter

We will start by discussing 1 of the most bizarre known cases that exist in criminal history. Charles Manson (fig.1), the Tate Labianca murders and the Manson family cult changed peoples ideas of what was possible. In particular the murder of Sharon Tate a beautiful shining star, who was also the pregnant wife of filmmaker and famous pedophile Roman Polanski.

The murders gave everyone another example that no one is safe or above the reach of the sticky tendrils of violence and degradation. In 1969 the United States was turned upside down by the startling discovery of a truly heinous series of murders at 10050 Cielo Dr.

The fears and doubts of many upstanding American citizens were now a reality. It appeared that the hippy drug culture and free love movements were dangerous after all or so they seemed to believe. The Manson family put the free love movement into a very negative light.

Draft dodgers, American soldiers returning from Vietnam, and middle to upper-class young people were leaving home or running away. Who knows what happened to most of them? What we do know is that some of them became caught up in some very greasy gears.

> "We are going to get up and scream. We are going to get up and burn an X in our heads."
> *–Patricia Krenwinkel*

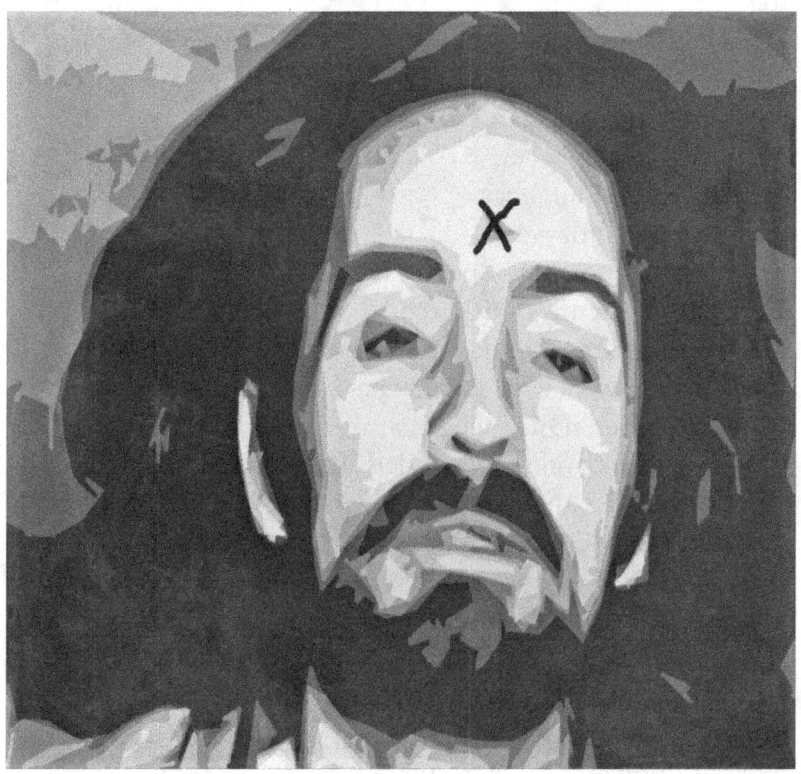

Fig. 1

Charles Manson
-AKA-
No Name Maddox
Charles Milles Maddox
Charles Hanson
Chuck Summers
Charles Miles Summers
Jesus Christ

God and country were expected to be holding the American family together. Times had changed. Americans opened their eyes and they saw the bogeyman. Manson and his legacy of brutality are only fear campaigns that drove

people to the heights of paranoia and confusion. The Manson family "a new model of living" did not exactly make sense to most folks. It is hard to tell how many people were ever actually part of the family. Manson gathered his followers from the bottom of the heap. The weak and the wounded. Throw away individuals who were either abandoned by their family or abandoned by society in one way or another.

The song Garbage Dump on Charlie's seminal album "LIE, The love and terror cult," (See Fig.2) reflects his attitude towards society and how people are often thrown away and then retrieved by Manson who gives them a new meaning and value to their lives.
The album was recorded in 1967 and released in 1970. The infamous trial was in full swing at the time that the LP dropped. Manson's glaring bulging-eyed stare graces the cover of the album. The image is probably the most well known iconic representation of Charles Manson. The recognizable Life magazine typeface is used on the cover creating the word Lie instead of Life. An apparent snub to the media and Manson's relentless argument that he was not responsible for the infamous murders that took place in 1969.

Manson being innocent is a real bone of contention for some people. On 1/25/1971 Manson was convicted of first-degree murder for directing the Tate Labianca murders. The idea is that since he did not physically commit the crimes he would not guilty of them. Just because Manson told these people to go out and kill does not mean that they had to. Sure we all have a choice but the people who committed those murders are being held responsible.

Manson ended up dismissing his lawyer Irving A. Kanarek and decided to represent himself. Probably not the best idea considering a pretty solid lack of evidence not based on testimony that Manson had instructed anyone to kill. A better legal team could have moved for a mistrial before the trial even began.

Part of the problem with this investigation has to do with the effect that the discovery of the truly horrible crime scene had on the first responders. Some mistakes were made that very well could have cost the prosecution the case today. The law enforcement agents involved acted out of confusion, disgust, and compassion. In the process they wreaked havoc on the Tate/Labianca crime scenes.

It is hard to blame them for their reaction but as professionals they should have secured the crime scenes properly. Securing the scene is the best thing they could have done for the victims. There have certainly been some horrible murders committed in America. The Villisca ax murder house, Lizzie Borden's parlor room, and Jeffery Dahmer's refrigerator are a few shining examples of human brutality.

The impact was similar in those cases. Being a criminal or law enforcement agent has to be pretty stressful. Take a moment to imagine getting the call on your radio to check up on a potential homicide or burglary.

The officers who received the code 2 on that beautiful California morning were being led down a path that they had never traveled before. 10050 Cielo Drive had become a charnel madhouse where no sense made sense. The officers called to the scene were not the first people to discover the demonic crimes that had occurred.

Perhaps the most unwitting person involved in this case was Winifred Chapman. Chapman worked as the Polanski's housekeeper. Winifred was dropped off at the property and went about her usual routine. As she was moving along her usual path Winifred starting seeing some bizarre signs that something very hinky might have occurred.

Chapman became the trumpeting herald of Helter Skelter. After following a trail of grim clues Chapman realized that there were pools of blood surrounding her. After seeing what she thought could have been a body Chapman went screaming from the property. In her fevered egress Winifred passed Steven Parent's car and saw his body.

We are going to take a quick intermission from this part of the story. I have prepared a short list of some of the things that made this case so strange some of the things that made the investigation so difficult, and some notable highlights of the trial. Hold tight we will pick up where we have left off a bit later.

A Short List

The crime scenes were not secured properly-

The absolute shock value of the murders clouded the judgment of the law enforcement agents involved.

1 Survivor-

The Cielo Drive estate caretaker was apprehended as the prime suspect in the murders. William E. Garretson was the only person found alive at Cielo drive on the morning of 8/09/69.

There are reports that Garretson was handled rather roughly by the Los Angeles police department. Garretson claimed to be completely oblivious of any of the mayhem that had ensued at Cielo Drive.

The police were not so sure about the honesty of those claims. Garretson was in such a state of confusion that he did not recognize his friend Steven Parent. Tex Watson had shot him in the face, rendering him much harder to identify. Parent was the inaugural victim of Helter Skelter.

Garretson said that Parent was the last person he had seen the previous evening. Garretson told the investigators that he was up all night listening to music, and writing letters. Garretson was put through the ringer, but his claims were eventually determined to be true or inconclusive.

Adversarial Process-

Both The Los Angeles Police Department, and the Los Angeles sheriff's department were put in charge of the case. Both of these agencies interpret the ritualistic manner of the murders in different ways.

The bizarre clues that were left behind became harder to fathom. Neither of these organizations were able to come up with any conclusions they could agree on. Coming to one-sided conclusions as individuals or a group primarily defines the adversarial process.

The adversarial process often occurs when there is a chance of a reward or greater recognition involved. Neither side wants to lose because that might make them seem inept.

The officers covered up the bodies-

When the law enforcement agents arrived they wrapped the bodies in white linen sheets. Abigail Folgers body was on the lawn for close to a week,

The sheets were left behind-

The white sheets used to cover the bodies were left behind. They did not make it to the morgue for analysis.

Blood splatter evidence was contaminated-
The officer in charge of securing the crime scene touched a bloody smudge on the front gate switch, creating a superimposition. The officer who fudged that bit of evidence admitted that he was in a panic to get out of there and away from that scene.

A boy found a gun-

A boy wandering in The Hollywood Hills found the
.22 caliber handgun used in the murder. After the
gun was turned in, it was not dusted for prints. The
gun was turned in 2 weeks after it was found.

Kicked pistol grip-

An officer kicked a part of the pistol grip from the
handgun found by the boy under a chair another
piece was kicked out of the front door. The piece was
broken off because the gun was used to bludgeon Jay
Sebring to death.

Blood samples not collected-

The forensic chemist involved with the crime scene
investigations did not collect blood samples from
some of the pools of blood at the crime scene. At
Cielo drive, Joe Granado did not collect blood
samples from the bodies in the yard or the living
room. At the Labianca residence, Granado did not
collect samples from the blood pools around the
victims because he assumed the blood belonged to
the victims.

21 out of 45-

For some reason that was never explained Granada did not test 21 of the 45 blood sample for subtypes. Subtype blood testing needs to be done very soon after the sample is collected. Otherwise, you can not determine the subtype of the blood sample because the properties of blood change quickly in a short time when exposed to oxygen.

Horn Rims-

A pair of horned rimmed glasses were initially found on the floor, and were then moved across the room onto a desk.

Difficult Re-Enactments-

The improper collection of forensic data, the crimes scenes not being secured properly, and the manipulation of objects directly related to the crimes made it very difficult to re-enact the murders.

Warrants not issued-

Arrest warrant were not issued for Manson or Atkins because they were already in custody. Warrants were issued for Kasabian, Krenwinkel, and Watson.

Footprints-

Investigators at the Cielo drive crime scene stepped in and tracked blood found at the front door through the residence. The shoes of the investigators had to be tested and identified to determine the investigator's footprints versus the assailants and the victims. One more error in an already chaotic scene.

Nixon-

A headline was released declaring President Nixon's verdict that Charles Manson was guilty. The declaration was made before Manson was found guilty in a court of law. There was a motion for a mistrial, but it was denied. Judge Holder made all of the jurors swear an oath not to allow Nixon's verdict to influence their own decision.

Loose Lips-

Susan Atkins confided some of the details of the murders and her participation in the crimes while she was in jail after being arrested at the Barker ranch. Susan Atkins became friends with a couple of career convicts. She felt comfortable enough with them to blab about the killings.

One of the things that she told them was that she had stabbed Sharon Tate and that she had tasted her blood. Atkins new found friends immediately snitched on Atkins. Susan's blabbing led to the arrests of Krenwinkel, Watson, Van Houten, and Kasabian.

No Motive -

Creating the body of evidence needed to prosecute Manson and the Family members involved in the murders proved to be very difficult. The motive for the killings was unclear.

Why had these people wreaked havoc on anyone? The robbery was quickly ruled out because the killers hardly took any substantial amount of the valuable items that were in both locations. There were so many similar clues that the crimes had to have a greater meaning.

Ronald Hughes-

On 03/29/1971, Ronald Hughes body was found wedged between some large rocks, in a gorge, by a fishermen in Ventura County California. Oddly enough this was the same day that Manson and the other co-defendants in the case were sentenced to death.

Ronald Hughes was the first public defender assigned to the case. Part of Manson's plan to escape guilt was to convince the courts that the family members who committed the helter skelter murders had acted independently and under their own motives.

Hughes had done a pretty good job discrediting Linda Kasabian. Hughes used Kasabian's claims of her being a witch, her belief in ESP, and her use of psychedelics in an attempt to symbolically destroy her. On the other hand Hughes was trying to paint Van Houten in an entirely different light.

Hughes was claiming that Van Houten had been under some mind control by Manson. Manson did not like this at all. The Manson family proceeded to throw the court into chaos.

The utter absurdity of the whole case boiled over once Atkins, Krenwinkel, and Van Houten declared that they wanted to testify. The girls wanted to take all of the blame and completely clear Manson. Hughes announced that he did not want to participate in the case. Van Houten was willing to testify against the council of Hughes, her lawyer. Manson was working both the offense and the defense of this case. In fact, Manson was directly influencing the case quite overtly at times. Hughes could not adequately defend Van Houten.

Hughes objected to his client taking the stand after Manson made his statement. At this point, Judge Older declared a ten-day recess so both sides could prepare the closing statements. Hughes never made it back to win the acquittal he was sure he could conjure for Van Houten. We will get to more of the meat on the bones of this incident a bit later. What I will say now is that some people feel that is quite evident that Hughes' demise was due to foul play. Manson and other members of the family made clear death threats to a few people during the trial. Manson's disapproval of Hughes' defense tactics was also well documented.

Hughes was known as the hippy lawyer, with this in mind and Hughes' reputation for being a free spirit it is not so strange to think a trip out to the wilderness might be what he needed to clear his mind. Hughes was camping in a well-forested area where there were many inherent pitfalls and dangers.

It just so happens during the time Hughes was camping in the area there were some mighty storms. The winds created high water and flash flooding. Hughes could have set his camp up in a sector that has been particularly sensitive to those natural dangers.

Of course that all sounds pretty tidy right? No... You are right it does not. Nothing about any of this is neat. We are going to move on to the next bizarre variable on our short list.

Irving Kanarek-

Kanarek was Hughes' replacement defender. Kanarek had a rather unsavory reputation. Kanarek started out in the aerospace field. Kanarek invented a corrosion inhibitor for North American Aviation.

The corrosion inhibitor was used for the Army's project Nike. Project Nike was a Bell Laboratories' proposal to create a line of sight anti-aircraft guidance system. Operation Nike was successful, and Bell Labs project was a reality. By the time Kanarek had gotten involved Project Nike had evolved to develop a whole lot more.

For some reason, Kanarek's security clearance was revoked in 1954. Kanarek was then fired from North American Aviation. Kanarek was around 34 years old at the time. In 1957 after some study, Kanarek was admitted to the California Bar.

Kanarek had worked on another high-profile case before The Manson Family trial. On 5/1/1968 Kanarek was petitioned to act as counsel for Jimmy Lee Smith. Smith was one of the people involved in the case that inspired the novel The Onion Field.

Kanarek was jailed twice during the Tate/Labianca proceedings. Judge Older placed him in contempt of the court on both occasions. In a sense, Kanarek was the perfect defender for Manson because of his courtroom shock tactics. Kanarek continually objected to almost everything throughout the trial. Kanarek had objected close to 200 times within the first couple of days of the trial.

Kanarek stuck it out to the end. Kanarek's 7-day long closing statement was an attempt to convince the jury that the girls who committed the murders did it for Tex Watson. Kanarek was pushing the idea that although Manson certainly was not an innocent man, he was not responsible for the Tate/Labianca murders.

Most of Kanarek's plan of attack and his final statements were seen in bad taste. Vincent Bugliosi gave Kanarek his due, by recognizing that Kanarek was simply doing his job as the defense. If Charles Manson was Jesus Christ, then Irving Kanarek was St. Peter. Of course, this is laughable, but I see a parallel. Kanarek was 100% dedicated to clearing Manson of any involvement in the Tate/Labianca murders.

Kanarek endured death threats, abuse, public ridicule, jail time, and character assassination. After the trial Kanarek fell under hard times. Kanarek had become both mentally disturbed and physically infirmed. Kanarek had a slow and hard downward spiral. After spending some time at the UCLA Medical Center for psychiatric treatment. Kanarek was fined by the State Bar for 3 claims made by former clients.

Some people guess all of Kanarek's misfortune is directly related to the Tate/Labianca trial. Even in a very non-metaphysical way it might be easy to understand how a case like that could wreck your physical and mental health. Kanarek, born 5/20/1920 is 96 years old and is still ticking away.

Barker Ranch Raid-

The family had been staying at two neighboring ranches between 1968 and 1969. The Barker Ranch was owned by relatives of Arlene Barker a Manson family member. The ranches in Death Valley were an ideal spot for the family.

Both locations were raided twice on consecutive days on 10/69. Local officials were initially making arrests for car theft and the destruction of an expensive piece of earth moving machinery. Manson was found jammed in a cabinet under the bathroom sink. The arrests made on those raids were the end of the line for the family.

Nobody likes a snitch-

Linda Kasabian was granted full immunity. Linda Kasabian drove to both the Tate and the Labianca murders. In both cases she was not directly involved in the killing as much as she was an unwitting participant. After the first night of helter skelter Kasabian claimed it was fear for her baby who was still in the Manson family day care at the time of the infamous murders.

Manson family values dictated that all children were everyone's children and no one was one person's mother or father. Kasabian and other parents were allowed periods of time with their children. The daycare was problematic for Kasabian who could not get to her daughter to escape.

After witnessing the Tate murders and dropping the killers off at the Labianca house. Kasabian fled without her child. She turned herself in 2 months after The Barker Ranch raid.

Kasabian's testimony was the nail in the coffin for Manson and the family concerning these crimes. Linda Kasabian became the star witness in the case. Kasabian was the Judas in this psychodrama.

Kasabian's innocence is still in doubt. Kasabian was an avid drug user and petty criminal. Linda may not have been a murderer but she certainly was not any more or less guilty of these crimes than anyone else involved under the terms of the law. Linda Kasabian's testimony was truly pivotal to the prosecution.

Kasabian's testimony was greeted with threats and general disdain from Manson and the family. After the trial Kasabian changed her identity and went into hiding.

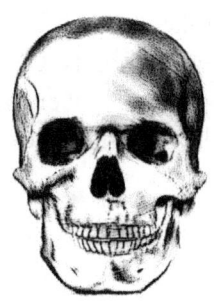

That was not such a short list after all. The initiation of helter skelter had some very weighty consequences. At the same time that Manson used the media to manipulate the events linked to the trial. The media managed the opinions and the facts of this case.

The media exaggerated a few facts about the case. The media peppered the story with a bit of misinformation. Journalist and the general public were rabid for information concerning the case. Everyone involved became a type of celebrity. The rumors that circulated about the crime scenes painted an even more heinous picture than the reality of them. The fear machine was running full throttle.

It is hard to believe as a society we want to take something terrible and imagine it to be even worse. The Tate/Labianca murder trial was truly one of the most bizarre cases in criminal history. RICO is one of the laws used to bring Manson down. The Racketeer, Influenced, and Corrupt Organizations act is the law that was created to prosecute and defend anyone involved in organized crime.

The origins of this law began in a plan to bring down mafia bosses and biker gang leaders. The law eventually expanded to the extent that it can be used to flush out crooked law enforcement agents and others who abuse their authority. On the other hand RICO can be used to protect law enforcement officials who expose these unlawful instances.

RICO is a law enacted in 1970 by the Organized Crime Control Act. RICO was enacted less than a year before Manson was convicted of all 7 counts of murder as a result of the vicarious liability rule and the joint liability rule of conspiracy. In another strange turn of events California decided to abolish the death penalty. Manson told Bugliosi that he felt like he had won considering that Bugliosi sent him back to prison. A place where Manson was completely comfortable.

Before we go any further I have to say that I am not writing this section of the book to either condemn or congratulate Charles Manson or the Manson family cult members that were involved or who still exist today. This section of the true crime chapter is necessary due to the offenses historical importance.

The crimes that occurred and the far-reaching repercussions of these events will not be aggrandized. Charles Manson, his devotees, and the media have done this enough. So much has been written discussed, analyzed and recorded concerning the Manson cult and the nature of their reputation that it almost seems redundant to write anything else.

I had originally intended to write about the Manson family trial and the circus sideshow that it became. Instead I have decided the best source of information concerning the trial is the book Helter Skelter. Anything I could write about that would just be paraphrased information from that source. So instead we are going to exit stage left and focus on the influence Manson still has, the murders, the conspiracies, and the paranormal ramifications of the killings.

How does it feel to be one of the beautiful people?

- THE BEATLES

Charles Manson drew some very creative parallels between himself and the original legendary boy band The Beatles. Manson's life experiences, the holy bible, and messages he believed he was receiving from The Beatles music are the underlying ideology, message, and warning of helter skelter.

On 01/1962 Tony Sheridan released his album My Bonnie. The Beatles were working with Tony Sheridan at the time. The Beatles had a different lineup. Ringo Star did not join the band until later. The Beatles were only on a few tracks of the album. Both Sheridan and The Beatles had become acquainted by playing some of the same nightclubs. The Beatles did not end up working with Sheridan long after that.

6 years later The Beatles released their self-titled album, which became known as The White Album. A year before that release, The Beatles released The Magical Mystery Tour. The Beatles released their Album Sgt. Peppers Lonely Hearts Club Band, only 6 months earlier. Their music had taken on some very distinct overtones. The Beatles, as a group, had started practicing transcendental meditation and experimenting openly with LSD.

The Beatles also developed a serious interest in Eastern philosophy. Of course at the time this was heresy. The Beatles are truly a legendary iconic band. Very much like Charles Manson and a few other influences. The Beatles were promoting the idea of breaking away from established norms and conventional ideas. It can even be argued that they were an actual catalyst in the era that defined a generation.

Of course the message The Beatles have for people is truly one of hope, love, and change through self-realization. Manson sold peace and love but delivered war and hate to the world. Later on in this section of the book we will discuss how Manson both directly and indirectly involved more than a few celebrities in his plans for helter skelter.

The Beatles became a symbol. A method to expand your mind. Many fans of The Beatles changed along with the band. The boys from Liverpool went from a relatively safe and familiar pop-rock type of sound to a much more colorful, gritty, confusing, and creative band. Manson was truly obsessed and possibly their biggest fan for better or worse.

The idea of helter skelter for The Beatles had very different motivations. A helter skelter is a mid-evil amusement park ride. In Britain, a helter skelter is a slide that winds around a tower. I am confident that most of us who grew up going to public schools may have experienced its modern counterpart.

Back in a time when people were less concerned about safety and more concerned with having fun. Recess areas and playgrounds usually contained a helter skelter of their own. The spiral slide. These hulking metal monstrosities were known for blistering your skin on a hot day and being the best slide to go down head first.

The Beatles decided to make a gritty song to respond to The Who. Helter Skelter is more or less a punk rock song about the fall of The Roman Empire. So yes Helter Skelter is a song about revolution and taking power back. The song remains valid when compared to any era. But it was not the kind of thing Manson made it out to be.

Since the birth of rock and roll the genre has been used as a scapegoat. Blaming behaviors and actions on something like rock and roll removes the responsibility of the individual. Elvis Presley, Jerry Lee Lewis, and Chuck Berry were all considered to be nothing less than heretical devils who were corrupting the youth of America. It is not just rock and roll that gets blamed, but film, literature, and video games as well. Ozzy Osbourne, Rob Zombie, and even the Judas Priest himself, Rob Halford, have been blamed. Blamed for something in connection with some act of revolution or violence. Marilyn Manson became connected to the killings at Columbine High School. The boys involved in the murders were big fans of the band. For better or for worse.

From what I understand this caused the individual Brian Warner, aka Marilyn Manson quite a bit of real emotional and psychological pain. Undeniably, insane people have found some straightforward messages hidden in the content of the artwork. The artwork typically is not intended to be interpreted in such a way. Vain attempts at gaining the attention of a celebrity have often ended in tragedy.

Mark David Chapman killed John Lennon thinking Jody Foster would be impressed. Nathan Gale murdered Dime Bag Darrel 24 years later on the same cold day in December. Gale believed he was justified in his action for a myriad of completely delusional reasons. What a waste of life. Both of these men had quite a bit more to give to the world. Stephen King and his wife have been attacked in their own home by a deranged fan.

George Harrison was attacked by a 33-year-old man from his hometown. Luckily Harrison and his wife survived. President Ford narrowly escaped death. Squeaky, one of the more infamous of the Manson girls attempted to assassinate Ford in 1975. Fromme was acting in response to peoples indifference to environmental pollution. Lynette was working on behalf of the environmental group ATWA.

There are more examples of crazed fans and zealots, holding their idols and causes to a greater degree than shared logic and reason dictate. In desperation and in an attempt to feel the power, gain control, or receive attention, many people have lost their lives.

So does this mean The Beatles and Marilyn Manson are responsible for the terrible things people did due to their influence? Some people would like for us to believe so. Dee Snyder went to war against Tipper Gore over censorship. Snyder did better than many people would have thought and delivered himself rather honorably in his pursuit of freedom and heavy fucking metal!

Many people would stand in the way of self-expression and art that is not geared towards what the consensus deems reality. All of the artists I have mentioned on these pages are all people who did just that. They delivered an alternative. Something that was not the same or safe.

There is an enormous amount of personal responsibility involved with life and art because they are a duality. Marilyn Manson has stated that if you as an individual are not raising your children then someone like him might be. Someone who understands and feels the same. Someone strong and charismatic who knows their value as an individual. Maybe even someone who can answer their questions, or who even asks them questions in the first place.

That idea was the ticket which Charles Manson used to ride down his kaleidoscope highway picking up hitchhikers along the way. So no, The Beatles and Marilyn Manson, are not responsible for the actions people have taken in a vain attempt to identify with them or become a part of their reality. Charles Manson believed he was enacting a plan hatched out by The Beatles to create a post-apocalyptic Garden of Eden.

The line is fine between the influence Manson has on his family, the influence The Beatles had on Manson, and then in return, the influence Manson had on The Beatles. Sometimes it is hard to know rather you should blame the knife or the hand that cuts you. I believe that the difference is the intention.

A gaming company Bethesda Gaming Studios, has made games like Fallout 4. Fallout 4 is a very realistic game that is full of potential for simulated violence. The game is set in a post-apocalyptic wasteland. Because Bethesda has created a game that simulates a post-apocalyptic world filled with terrifying dangers and scenarios does not mean they want the world to end.

Manson wanted these people to go out and kill directly. There was no real gray area in his intentions at least concerning these murders. Other than potentially not knowing who was going to be murdered. Manson knew what he wanted. So Manson is responsible for the influence he has and has had on his followers.

Each member of The Beatles had their disgusted reaction to Charles Manson. The Beatles were acquainted with both Sharon Tate and Roman Polanski. The Beatles were appalled at the outcome of these events. Just like the way Charles Manson killed the 60's, he made The Beatles take a more discriminating look at their work and the influence they were having on the world as a whole.

George Harrison was terrified that his song Piggies directly influenced some of the violence in both the Labianca and Cielo drive murders. Paul McCartney's mind was blown because of how Manson related the song Helter Skelter to the book of revelations and the four horsemen of the apocalypse. Manson believed they had a particular message for him.

I guess this might make sense in a way if you take into account that Manson believed he was Jesus Christ. From the White Album, Manson gathered that he was the returned Christ. Manson believed the song Revolution #1 was a Que for Manson to reveal his message. Manson also found he was supposed to explain his message in the medium of an album.

Manson foretold of war that would arise over racial tensions. Black people would rise against white people and an apocalyptic event would occur. Manson, feeling like he was in the know because he was Jesus Christ prophesied that he would lead his people into safety. For this purpose Manson gathered quite a few dune buggies and other vehicles to escape into remote locations in the desert.

In the end, Manson and the family would wait it out until things settled down. When the time was right Manson would reveal himself as the lord and savior of this new world. All sounds pretty tidy. Hey, why not, it could work. Right? It all seemed pretty believable to Manson and his followers.

The problem was that things just were not lining up the way they were supposed to. Manson wanted to become more famous than The Beatles. All of the channels Manson had forced open in the music industry had dried up and closed off to him. Manson was just too much lemonade for these guys to swallow. After the final rejection, Manson was furious.

What the hell did Charles Manson want to achieve? In a way, I think he just wanted to be a rock star. Much like Hitler Manson was a failed artist who was shunned and ridiculed by his peers. In the book The Gates of The Necronomicon the author Simon refers to Manson as being the kind of victim society does not like. Manson did not keep his head down and become rehabilitated. The only thing he apologizes for is not killing more people.

Manson refuses to step in line. Even though his plans on how he was going to spread the message did not seem to be manifesting helter skelter was coming down fast. Other than Manson's desire for revenge against Terry Melcher, the system, and his ultimate disappointment over his failed record deal things were not adding up. The fate of the victims had been sealed.

Just like in any tangled web, there was a series of bizarre events that lead the family to Cielo drive. The discovery of the body of a member of the Black Panther Party really put a bug in Manson's bonnet. Let's push on, forward to the bloody end. The wheel spins and helter skelter begins its crazy carnival ride down a spiral nose dive.

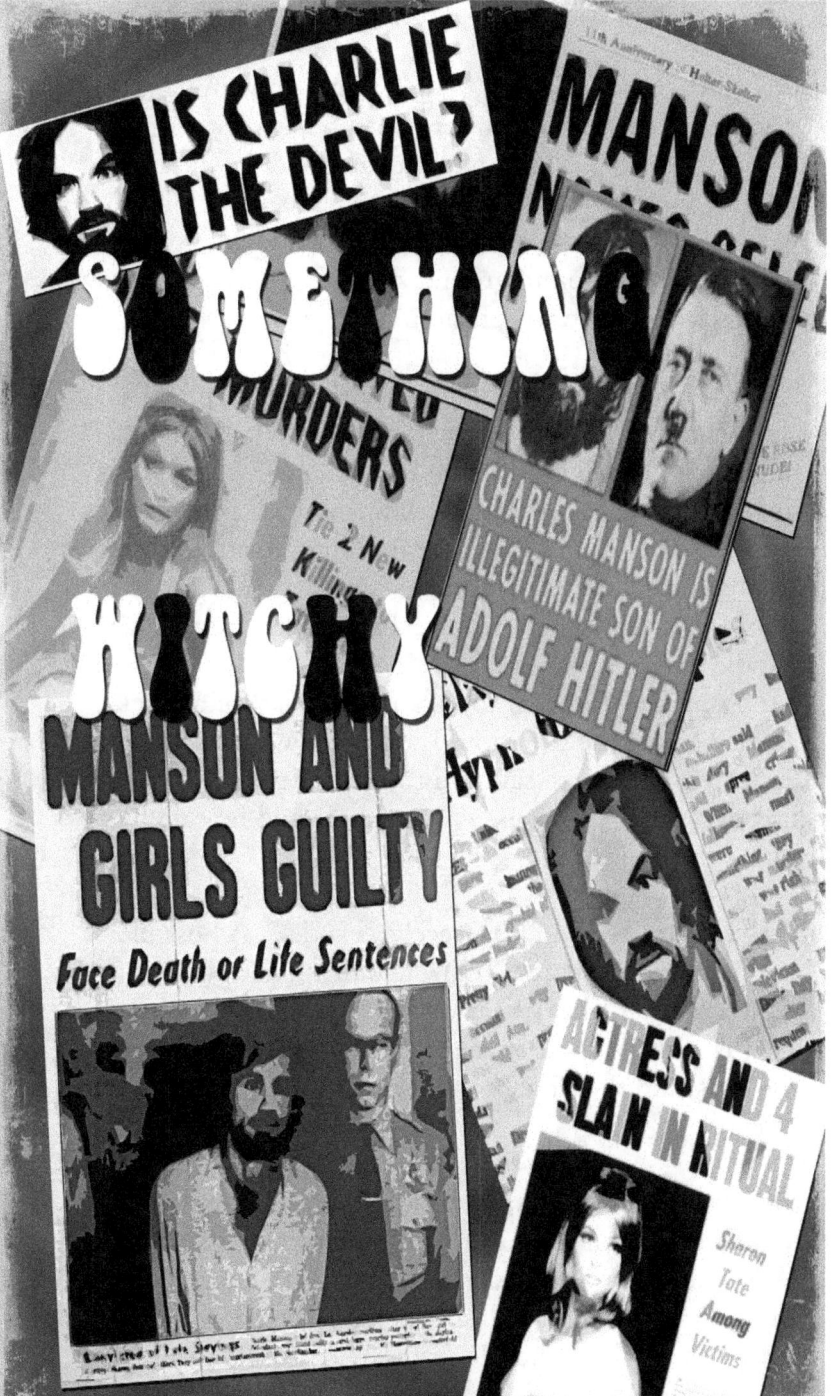

On 08/08/1969, Charles Manon cast a powerful and destructive spell. Manson sent his disciples out with the intent to murder. Manson instructed Watson, Susan Atkins, and Patricia Krenwinkel, to leave something witchy in their wake. Kasabian chauffeured Manson's murderous children to ground zero of helter skelter. Now, let's pick up where we left off in chapter 1.

"Murder, death, bodies, blood!" Screamed Chapman as she beat a tattoo into young Jim Asin's door. Asin was outside by the car at the time Chapman appeared at his door. It just so happened that Jim Asin was a member of a boy scout law unit. Jim was mindful of his training and recorded the time of Chapman's arrival at 8:33 a.m. Mr. Asin Jim's father answered the door and tried to get a handle on the situation.
Mr. Asin and Jim went to Polanski's house for a quick assessment of the situation. The Asin's saw the same cut wires Chapman saw and the Rambler sitting in the driveway. The Asin's wisely went home and repeatedly called the police.

9:14 a.m. unit 815 and 816 receive a code 2. A possible homicide reported at 10050 Cielo drive. The authors of Helter Skelter, The True Story of The Manson Murders, say that this is where there is some confusion, concerning the calls, and the time of the arrival of the first responding officers.

Derosa who arrived first testified that he arrived at 9:05 a.m. The original code 2 was dispatched at 9:14 a.m. Whisenhunt proved to arrive between 9:14 and 9:25 a.m. Burbridge, who arrived last testified to being on site at 8:40 a.m. Bugliosi and Gentry were correct. Things got more confusing from that point on.

Derosa was doing his best to interview Winifred Chapman. Chapman was not able to make any real coherent statements at the time. All she could get out was the helter skelter mantra, "Murder, death, bodies, blood!" Chapman is probably fortunate that her mind was not able to organize the ultra-violence that was in her periphery.

The things that she saw in the corners of her eyes were no longer recognizable to her as people. Even though she was familiar with all of the victims, she was not able to identify any of them in her interview. Chapman went back to the house on Cielo drive one last time. After Sharon Tate's funeral Chapman testified to cleaning the word Pig off of the door.

11/06/1969, Chapman was found after she had gone missing for over 2 weeks. The details are sketchy, but she did not want any more involvement with the case. Chapman was treated for shock at the UCLA medical center. It is possible to imagine that slowly over time her mind was able to process what she had seen. I am sure those revelations were truly apocalyptic.

Derosa was having no luck with Chapman other than adding Jay Sebring into the equation. Mr. Asin stepped in again with some helpful info. Asin was able to let Derosa know that the Polanski's had been renting the property from Rudi Altobelli. Asin also told them about William Garretson who was the caretaker of the building. Garretson was staying in the guest house. A picture was starting to develop. The negative was burning away and the proof was about to be revealed.

Things were moving quickly. Derosa retrieved his weapon from his squad car and had Chapman advise him on how to operate the entry gate of the property. Derosa made it to Steven Parent's Rambler just about the time that officer Whisenhunt arrived at the bottom of the drive. After meeting up with Whisenhunt and confirming the possible code 2 they both headed up the drive together.

On the second trip up the drive the officers made some observations concerning Parent and his car. (See Fig. 3) After a search nothing else surfaced in this area. Right about now officer Burbridge arrives and meets up with the other patrolmen. All 3 of the men leave the area together. The officers then discover 2 bodies. The officers describe the scene as being very surreal against the backdrop of the beautifully manicured and landscaped yard.

The view from the property was amazing. In the midst of a quiet magically green swimming pool and the silent vigil of an old wishing well time had stopped. The bodies were utterly brutalized. The amount of carnage unleashed on these poor souls was unbelievable. The first body: Wojciech Frykowski, was stabbed 51 times by Watson. (See Fig.4)

Abigail Folger was the next tortured spirit to be discovered. Folger had managed to escape out of a bedroom into the pool area momentarily. Krenwinkel caught her, threw her to the ground and stabbed her to death, together with Watson who joined in. Abigail Folger was stabbed up to 28 times. The officers initially thought she was wearing a red nightgown, but it was just soaked through in her blood. (See Fig. 5)

Fig. 3 Steven Parent's Car

Steven Parent was mentioned earlier on the "short list." Steven Parent was at the wrong place at the wrong time. Steven parent became the first victim of helter skelter. It is very bizarre that Parent was involved in all of this madness. The popular opinion is that Parent was there to sell Garretson a clock radio. Tex Watson shot Parent while parent was sitting in his car. Later that day, Winnifred Chapman would run screaming past his body.

Steven Parent

Fig. 4 Voytek Frykowski

Fig. 5 Abigail Folger

All 3 of the officers started to become unnerved by the scene. They were under suspicion that assailants or a lone psycho were still on the premises. All of this was so out of place on that beautiful California morning. At this point the 3 men split up. Derosa hung back with the bodies on the lawn. Entering the house was the next course of action for Whisenhunt and Burbridge.

The officers decided the front door might not be the best choice for their purposes. In search of the Northern part of the house, they found that a screen had been removed from a window. Closer inspection revealed a slit in the screen. The officers deduce that this was the way the killer (s) entered the house. Eventually the officers entered an open window and stepped into a freshly painted room. Since a baby was on the way I imagine the room was to be used as a nursery.

Meanwhile,Derosa went to take a look at the front door area. What caught his attention were the pools, splatters, splashes, and puddles of blood, that soaked the entire area. It took Derosa a moment to notice the word pig written in blood on the door.

Making it through the door, Derosa makes a turn and sees the horned rimmed glasses and pieces of the broken gun butt which were eventually moved and kicked out of their original spots. 2 things that created a lot of confusion later on in the investigation.

The 3 officers met up in the area of the house close to the door but outside of the foyer. Burbridge and Whisenhunt had moved from the bedroom to the kitchen and dining room to meet up with Derosa. The day that these men converged in this chamber to witness this atrocity should have been a day that they phoned it in and stayed home sick.

The officers had gone from a possible homicide to 3 confirmed deaths and so many questions naturally they became a little confused. These men were regular patrolmen they were not hardened detectives who had witnessed anything like this before. The thing is it was not over yet. The officers noticed a huge American flag draped across the back of an equally large couch.

The men found Sharon Tate on the other side of that sofa.(See Fig. 5) Just like all of the other victims she had been utterly brutalized. Tate was pushed back against the couch in a fetal position. A white rope was wrapped around her neck strung between the rafters of the ceiling and connected on the other end to Jay Sebring. Following the line to its grizzly end was where they first noticed Sebring's blood-soaked body.

The death toll mounts drastically. The body count jumped to 5 confirmed deaths. In the book Helter Skelter The actual story of the Mason Murders, on page 8. The authors say that "None of the officers thought to check either body for a pulse." The victims had been so thoroughly massacred that it was quite evident they were no longer in the land of the living.

Fig. 5 Sharon Tate and Jay Sebring

*Sebring & Tate on better days. At a
point in time, Sebring & Tate were a couple.
Even though they broke up, they
remained great friends.*

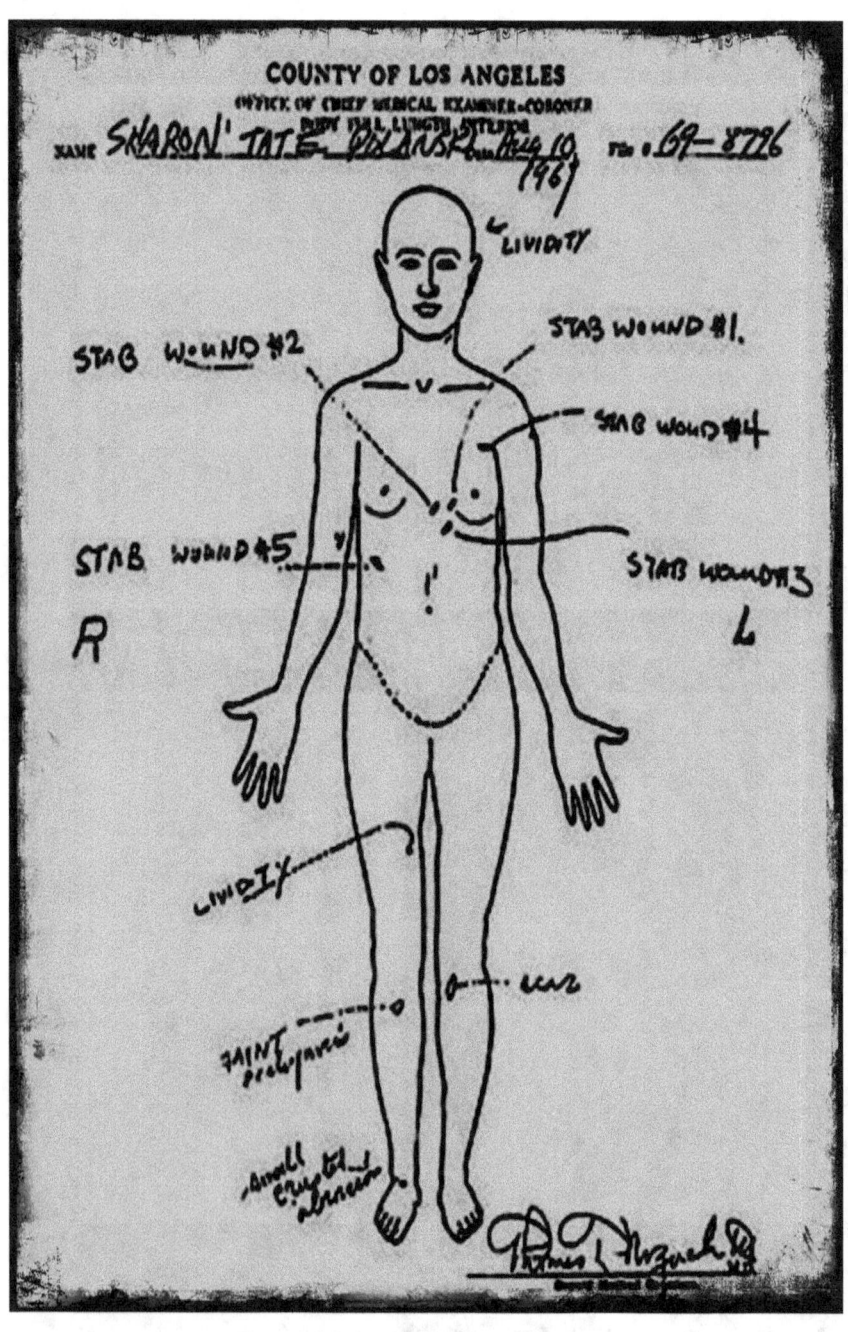

Sharon Tate's autopsy sheet illustrates the true brutal savagery of her murder.

The night before the beginning of the helter skelter murders William Garretson sat in the guest house. The guest house was maybe a little over 100 feet from the main house on Cielo drive. Garretson did not know it, but he was waiting for Steven Parent to show up with a clock radio Garretson might have been interested in buying.

Steven wanted to save money for college so he was trying to make as much cash together as he could. Parent was out cruising in his fathers white Dodge Rambler. It was a nice quiet night in the Hollywood Hills. Parent and Garretson had become acquainted after Parent picked Garretson up hitchhiking.

Parent drops by hangs out for a while and then gets shot in the driveway by Watson on his way to his next destination. At this point Garretson claims he was up for the rest of the night writing letters and listening to music. A little digging has shown that some people are very doubtful about the validity of all of Garretson's claims. Understandably it is unbelievable Garretson was so close to being a victim of helter skelter but somehow avoided death.

There is some speculation that Parent and Garretson were better acquainted than the press let on. A vehicle matching the description of Steven Parent's Rambler was spotted parked on Cielo Drive a couple of days earlier. I guess this would not seem strange if not for Garretson's polygraph test coming back inconclusive.

Garretson answered some very personal questions while undergoing his polygraph exam. One of the things that makes this case so fascinating is all of the little details. Sometimes it seems the atrocities committed that night are often throwing a shadow over the other real life stuff that was going on there already.

Maybe Parent and Garretson had a relationship of some kind. Today that does not seem strange but at the time, the idea would not sit well with many people. It is possible Garretson and Steve were also just buddies and they got high and then Parent split. Steven could have been dropping off some drugs for Garretson.

The police reported that Garretson seemed to be in the residual state of narcotics. Garretson could have been coming down off of a trip or something. Maybe Garretson had some drugs for Parent or perhaps Parent just came to sell a clock radio to Garretson who was high and bisexual but never had sex or used drugs with Parent.

It's like I have said. Life was happening on Cielo Drive before Manson's curse and the family snuffed it out. Other than just including this information to be conclusive and well-rounded. I do not see why any of that matters one way or the other. All of the victims and the killers all had lives before that day and were involved in whatever their lives entail. In any case Garretson was the sole survivor.

Rather he was hiding and hoping not to be found or he was oblivious to what was going on outside of the range of his high-fidelity stereo. Garretson's attorney advised him against talking about any sex or drugs which might have been involved. There are claims that some narcotics were found in Sebring's car. So yes there is much more to this whole case than we know.

OK, back to that beautiful August morning. The officers ended up searching the rest of the house. They come out of the house by the pool area. The bright glare coming off of the swimming pool blinds all 3 of the men. In the stillness of the morning they hear the only sound they did not create shatter the silence. Garretson the property caretaker was in the guest house with his dog.

The officers get organized to bust in on who they believed, was the deranged psychopath responsible for all of the carnage they had witnessed that morning. The officers bust in on Garretson who is more than a little caught off guard. Garretson's dog charges and the patrolmen manage to subdue the dog and Garretson. Garretson is taken into custody and released a short time later. The media storm happens almost instantly. LA is about to be rocked to its foundations. The brutality continues with the Labianca murders. The same type of message was expressed at their home.

We are not going to pursue the course of these events any further. I have only added this bizarre account of what happened to paint the picture. The rest of the tale is directly related to the connections between all of the people involved. The list is long and varied.

Since we are focusing on the Cielo Drive murders, I am not going to be elaborating on the Labianca killings. Bugliosi and Gentry's book contain all of those details. For now we are going to take another turn on our journey. Let's get off this crazy thing! We are going to take a look at Bugliosi and Gentry's book. As can be expected Charles Manson generates a massive wave of pop and cult media culture. So there is no shortage of material in this area. Charles Manson is idolized and celebrated by many. Manson seems to have as many fans as detractors.

We are going to get caught up with a few members of the Manson family. Where are they now? What did they do? How involved were they in the overall scheme of things? Charles Manson is still a master of shock value. I am going to introduce some of the characters who are involved. As goes the way of many overused symbols the meaning that sustains them is usually lost and convoluted over time. These murders have had a far-reaching and varied effect. For now let us explore Charles Manson as a pop culture icon and as a movement unto himself.

POP Super mega sensation Manson

The Star Killer & Pop Culture Icon

The book Helter Skelter was written in 1974 by Vincent Bugliosi and Curt Gentry. Bugliosi was the prosecuting attorney in The Manson Family trial. Curt Gentry was an author who produced a few notable works. Both Bugliosi and Gentry have passed away. Gentry in 2014, and Bugliosi in 2015. Both men had great careers and the book Helter Skelter was only 1 chapter in their lives.

Bugliosi spent 8 years in the Los Angeles County district attorneys office. Vincent had quite a knack when it came to getting his job done. In the time he spent in that office, he successfully prosecuted 105 of 106 felony jury trials. Inside of those numbers, he also had 21 murder convictions without ever losing.

In 1972 Bugliosi left that office and started his private practice. Along with writing a few other books, he wrote a book concerning his outrage over the OJ Simpson trial and the Murders of Nichole Brown and Ronald Goldman called, "Outrage: The 5 reasons OJ Simpson got away with murder."

The book Helter Skelter for short is a true crime account of the killings of Leno and Rosemary Labianca, Sharon Tate, Abigail Folger, Jay Sebring, and Wojtek Frykowski. The crime itself has been more or less abbreviated to the Tate Labianca Murders. Helter Skelter is also an account of the Manson family members involved with the murders and their prosecution.

The book also entails some of the activities related to the Manson family and how Charlie gathered his children together in a pied piper fashion, and some of their beliefs concerning the world as a whole. Helter Skelter quickly became a best-selling novel. In 1975 Helter Skelter won the Edgar award for best true crime book. Helter Skelter has had many reprints since the originals came screaming off of the presses in 1974.

The book is known as the most successful true crime book ever written. To this date, 20,000,000 copies of Helter Skelter have scarred, and opened the minds, of people of all varieties across the world. Hell, maybe even the multiverse. Who knows? Not me. In 1976 Helter Skelter hit the small screen in a made for television adaptation of the book.

In 2004 a remake of Helter Skelter was released. This version seemed to focus on Manson. On 5/28/15, the television series Aquarius debuted on NBC. The show is a period crime drama created by John McNamara. Aquarius is a highly dramatized account depicting some true, some fabricated, and other speculated events concerning the Manson family and Charles Manson.

The Show Stars David Duchovny as hard-hitting Samson Benedictus, also known as Hodiak. Charles Manson is portrayed by Gethin Anthony. Some of the members of the Manson family and Charlie have attracted quite a bit of media exposure. Manson and some of his known machinations had saturated pop culture and inspired more than a few artists to invoke Manson to add terror and tension to their art.

Marilyn Manson created an archetype based off of the duality of Charles Manson, and Marilyn Monroe. In this case Marilyn Manson was using symbols of both of the best and the worst parts or the prettiest and the ugliest aspects of a period.

Manson uses the irony and the tragedy of these two symbols to convey ideas that represent these figures to create an atmosphere for his artwork. Of course anyone who is familiar with the self-proclaimed Antichrist and time traveler's artwork knows it has very dark overtones which are often filled with esoteric symbolism.

In the pilot episode of MTV's Celebrity Death Match, Marilyn Manson battled the more mysterious aspect of this dichotomy when he squared off against Charles Manson in a battle royal to the death. Marilyn Manson overcame Charles Manson by reaching into Charlie's mouth and pulling his skeleton through Charlie's gaping orifice.

Ice Cube gives Charlie a shout out in the N.W.A song Straight Outta Compton. Rob Zombie has used quite a bit of sampled bits and serial killer slogans in his music. Including White Zombie's version of Children Of The Grave and Real Solution #9. Charles Manson seems to inspire fear and has become a symbol of death, revolution, and sudden or unexpected change.

At the same time that he inspires fear in many he seems to inspire hope in some. Manson has been popularized and celebrated as a way for a network to get their ratings up. Manson and some of the members of the family have appeared on interviews with more than a few notable journalists on probably most major networks at some point in time. Everybody wants to tune in and get a little slice of the chaos and insanity that Manson oozes.

Off of the top of the list would be Barbara Walters, Diane Sawyer, and Geraldo Rivera. Each of this journalist gave what they depicted as a twisted view into the mind of a maniac. Of course people ate it up and the broadcasts concerning Manson are known for super high ratings and the journalists involved, consider these interviews to be milestones in their careers.

Many people have taken more than a passing interest in Charles Manson and the Tate Labianca murders. Countless websites are revolving specifically around these crimes. The product is the cult of the cult. Many people have tried to capture Manson's charisma and use it to their ends. One thing that is for sure is that there are plenty of individuals who want to be controlled. Manson happens because people allow it.

You can go on a tour to Death Valley to visit and explore the infamous site: The Spawn ranch. There is not much left there except for blasted ruins. On quiet days and nights can you hear the family singing along with Charlie? I am sure there are ghosts so I know that there are probably plenty of memories locked there in time.

You can take a 3-hour tour and visit all of the sites involved if you wish. Paranormal investigators, true crime buffs, the morbid, and the deranged have visited Cielo drive only come back with diverse experiences. People visit most often on the anniversary of the murders.

The house was built in 1944. The French actress Michele Morgan had the house constructed by an architect named J.F. Wadkins. The house was erected in the style of a 19th-century farmhouse. There were quite a few celebrities that spent some time in the house before Polanski and Tate moved in.

Carey Grant spent his honeymoon at the house after he married Dyan Cannon. Henry Fonda, Paul Revere and the Raiders, and Terry Melcher all lived at the house before Sharon Tate and Roman Polanski. Manson's first visit to the house is believed to be during the time that Melcher lived on the property.

Trent Reznor lived in and worked in the house. Reznor recorded the album The Downward Spiral on the property. Reznor moved in sometime in 1992. Trent referred to his studio at the house as Le Pig. Reznor cranked out quite a bit of his best work in the place.

The Broken EP was recorded here as well along with the video for a song called Gave Up. Marilyn Manson's seminal album Portrait of An American Family was also recorded at Le Pig. It seems that there was some paranormal activity occurring on the property. There are rumors of strange problems with equipment and recording devices.

It seems that a chance encounter with Sharon Tate's sister got Reznor thinking. Trent moved out in 1993 because there was just too much history there for him to deal with. As a memento he kept the front door. Shortly after he left the house it was demolished.

It is true this tale is twisted and tragic beyond reason. It is not a surprise the house on Cielo Drive was destroyed. The act seems to be a way to bury the past or an attempt to heal the blasted ground. Charles Manson has had quite the impact on our world. The book Helter Skelter, all of the television shows, pop culture iconography, and countless devotees of Charlie will not let this rest.

Is it worse for a celebrity to die or to be murdered? No, it is just harder to believe that the people we put on pedestals will ever fall. How can they when they have been immortalized? That was the rub of Manson. No one is safe anywhere. In one unfortunate turn the family flipped the worlds of many people upside down. We lost a beautiful talented actress and a few other individuals who were unceremoniously flung to a brutal demise.

Understandably Manson does not have many supporters but he has a few. Some people feel that the Manson family has been operating the whole time Charlie has been in prison. The ones who did end up incarcerated have more or less recanted their crimes and some seem to have developed a higher spiritual calling.

Susan Atkins had such an experience. Before dying on 9/24/09, Atkins was married twice, received regular conjugal visits, and was denied parole 18 times. The Governator of California, Arnold Schwarzenegger denied Sexy Sady's compassionate release request in an eye for an eye manner.

(See Fig 3) Atkins also filed a lawsuit stating that she was a political prisoner and that she should have been paroled. Before she died in 2009 she racked up a considerable welfare debt equaling close to or over 1,850,000. Bugliosi stated that the only reason she should be released is too severe the cost of her welfare debt and her burden on the state.

Charles "Tex" Watson has had a bit of a less exciting time in prison. So far Tex has been denied parole 14 times. Tex is up for parole this year, 2016 in November.

Catherine Share, who is one of the family members not associated with the infamous murders was an avid recruiter for Manson. Share has been particularly enamored by Charlie.

Share and a few other family members were arrested and charged with conspiracy to attempt to dissuade a witness from testifying. Share was planning on dosing Barbara Hoyt with a lethal dose of LSD.

Hoyt was a family member who testified against the family.

In 08/71 Share robbed a surplus store with Mary Brunner and some other members of the family. By the time the police arrived, they had stolen about 150 guns. Share drew down and opened fire on the police resulting in a serious gunfight. Share was shot and taken into custody.

It is believed that they were getting the guns to stage a hostage crisis,by hijacking an airplane so that they could bargain for Manson's release. After her release from prison 4 years later she found Jesus and abandoned her allegiance to the Manson family.

Bobby Beausoleil, the man who stabbed Gary Hinman to death and wrote political piggy on the wall in Hinman's blood is still sitting in prison. His last parole meeting was in July of 2015. **Paul Watkins,** died of leukemia in 1990. Watkins was in Los Angeles at the time of his death. Watkins was not on board with helter skelter but felt a larger than life attraction to Manson. Once he heard of the Tate Labianca murders, he turned states evidence against Manson and the family.

Sandra Good AKA "Blue", moved to Hanford, California after she completed her parole in 1985, to be closer to the prison where Charlie sat. On 03/16/79, Blue was charged with conspiracy to send threatening letters through the mail. The letters were connected to death threats sent to 170 Corporate executives. After her release from prison she still claims her allegiance to Manson and the family.

The original Manson girl, **Mary Brunner** is the mother of one of Manson's children. Charlie and Mary drifted around for a while before they started developing the family. Brunner was cleared of any responsibilities for the Tate Labianca killings but she was at the robbery with Catherine Good. Brunner was released in 1977 and is supposed to be living anonymously somewhere in Middle America.

Figure 3

What you are looking at is the picture of Arnold, and Atkins along with a few other people. Arnold was visiting the Sybil Brand Institute for Women. The picture started appearing on the Internet after The Governator himself denied Atkins appeal for compassionate release from prison in 2008.
This picture was taken way before Arnold was the governor of anything except his biceps. This pic is only one of the many strange synchronicities that are involved in all of this. Manson and a few members of the family crossed paths with influential people.

When **Leslie Van Houten** was 19 she stabbed Rosemary Labianca 16 times. Leslie seems to have been thinking that this act was helping to kick off helter skelter. Van Houten's parole has been denied over and over again. On 09/07/17 Van Houten was granted parole. **Linda Kasabian** and her daughter moved into Spahn ranch in 7/69. Linda was totally smitten by Manson. Less than a month later she sat outside in the car at the house on Cielo drive while Sharon Tate and everyone else was being murdered around her. Linda testified against the family. She avoided prison and moved to the East Coast. Last she was seen Linda was living in a trailer park with not much to show for her life. I think it is safe to say that **Lynette Fromme** has to be Charles Manson's biggest fan. Lynette known as Squeaky, had to be one of the most devoted members of the family. While the Manson trial was taking place she camped outside of the courthouse.

After his conviction, Squeaky would follow Manson from prison location to prison location. Fromme would live in the area until Manson was transferred to a different penitentiary. The secret service apprehended Fromme when she pulled a gun on President Ford in 1975. After being sentenced to life in prison she escaped in 1987. Lynette was captured again but released in 2009. Squeaky could be anywhere doing anything.

Charles Manson, died on 11/19/17. Manson corresponded with quite a few people on the outside and still has what seems to be a strong following even after death but a little less hype. Manson himself has said that he never wanted to leave prison but I doubt that is true.

Charlie died in the Bakersfield, California hospital. Manson probably lived more than two-thirds of his life in the system. One thing that is for certain is that he sure tried to get a lot done when he was not in prison.

Not all of the members of the family went to jail. Some of them scattered across the empty spaces. Many wanted to bury themselves in obscurity and distance themselves as far as their minds and bodies could carry them from their questionable pasts. Some probably still hold onto to their old ideas and very well might live lives that reflect those ideals. The Manson cult is alive and well. More often than not I wonder what it is that truly attracts people to Manson.

Is it the same thing that repulses others? It easy to relate to someone like Charles Manson on a surface level. Many people relate to the attitude of Charles Manson. Just be yourself. Leave out the bullshit and learn what you can from a person like Charles Manson. There are just so many examples of times were people have just let themselves be led into some of the most horrible things you can imagine. I am sure it has happened to each of us at one time or another. In the next chapter we are going to spend some pages looking at some of the people and groups who have supported Manson and the level of influence he had on the outside world.

Sympathy For The Devil

You might find it hard to believe but there are quite a few criminals who have very avid fan clubs, supporters, and admirers. As I mentioned Susan Atkins was married twice and had many conjugal visits. Richard Ramirez also managed to get hitched. Ted Bundy had loads of marriage proposals pouring in from all over the place.

One of his biggest new Manson fans seems to be a women named Star. Afton Burton uses the Manson given name and has become known in the media as Star. Star had been in communication with Manson since she was 17 years old. Star believes that Manson is innocent of the charges of the crime. Burton also believes that Manson is a political prisoner.

Star maintains websites for Manson and is a member of the environmental group ATWA. The acronym stands for air, trees, water, and animals. The group's main concerns revolve around protecting the environment, maintaining a strict philosophy, and making sure Manson is portrayed and represented correctly. The ATWA website is choco block of information concerning Manson, Manson's environmental and spiritual philosophies, and the beliefs and ideals of the group.

The goals and ideas of ATWA are based on the ideals set forth by The Civilian Conservation Corps. From 1933 to 1944 Franklin D. Roosevelt developed the New Deal, and a man named Robert Fechner headed the agency. The New Deal was a system devised in response to the great depression.

These devices focused on what are known as the 3 R's, relief, recovery, and reform. The principles set forth were designed to help defeat a depression and contribute to stabilizing an economy. The program was initially set up for single men raging between the ages of 18-23. A short period later the group included 17-28-year-olds.

The idea was to give unskilled labor jobs to these men concerning the development and conservation of natural resources on state, local, and federally owned land. Thus creating employment in the time of a depression while cultivating, and harvesting natural resources at the same time! Not a bad idea. About 3,000,000 young men were involved in this program.

One of the core ideas of ATWA is that anything that sins against the air is a sin against your life. It seems that Manson was inspired to protect the environment by witnessing the slow and steady spread of electricity in the small rural communities where he grew up. Not everyone wanted to have electricity because it represented a loss of independence and a way to force people to conform to what society sees as acceptable.

According to the ATWA site Manson noticed that every time he got out of jail or prison more of the natural environment had been taken over by progress. The website also has updates from Manson, videos, pictures, a store, information, and even evidence that points to the fact that the Manson was trial was unfair and biased. Star's primary concern seemed to be putting together enough information to force a retrial for Manson.

ATWA also has ways you can get involved with the group. One option is to start a cleanup project in an area or a particular location. You can donate to the organization. There are some ideas concerning how you can help make changes yourself. You can also get involved with the savior project. The project includes using a seed gun device to shoot organically designed seed pods to reforest deforested areas.

Yes, all of this seems really great! Is it possible that the collective will of Manson and the people involved in this group are yielding positive results? It appears to be the case. Even though the message seems clear some of the group's ideas, and philosophies bend towards what resembles Eco terrorism. A few of the ideas that are thrown around allude to cultist behavior. Considering what is known about Manson and his philosophies, definitely makes it hard to see this in a positive light.

Is ATWA just the family with a fresh coat of paint, and a focus on more of an ecological war on society? The idea is a part of their value system. Manson has always had a bone to pick with progress. In any case as of now there is no known evidence of the group doing anything that does not reflect their constitutional rights.

If you know about Star you probably know her as Charles Manson's fiancée. The couple received their marriage license on 11/07/14. Most of the events associated with their union have been reported in a tabloid like fashion which seems to be the only way news about Manson is ever reported. I believe this is due simply to the sensationalism of Manson,

There are a few reasons that have been proposed to explain why Star wants to marry Charlie. One is that Star loves him. Another being that if Star is Manson's wife she could have gained access to information she needed to help Manson get a new trial. Still 1 motive that has been tossed around is that Star wants to take ownership of Manson's body after his death so that it can be displayed as something touristy for fans and other maniacs alike.

Apparently Manson thought that was ridiculous because he was pretty sure that he was never going to die. Charlie also reported that all of this is simply a design created for media consumption. That sounds like something he might say. Star also maintains a website dedicated to collecting letters to encourage the retrial of Manson. I guess there is no point in doing this now. Along with Star and ATWA people are running Manson forums all over the Internet. Manson has a pretty significant cyber presence. Not all of the sites and forums are pro Charlie. The more we dig the deeper we get.

Nikolos Schreck is an author, filmmaker, and musician. In 1984 Schreck fronted and founded the collective known as Radio Werewolf. Schreck also co-lead a magical school referred to as The Werewolf Order with Zeena Lavey Schreck. Nikolos leads a rather interesting life and has a unique perspective on the world. Schreck has made a documentary about Charles Manson and all of the things related to helter skelter called: Charles Manson Superstar.

Schreck has also published a book called The Manson File: Myth and Reality of An Outlaw Shaman. The well-researched account digs into Charles Manson's philosophies, the occult, spiritual beliefs, and Manson's involvement with environmental movements and concepts. He attempts to paint Manson in a different light.

Schreck also thinks Manson was a kind of a patsy and a pawn in a much larger conspiracy. The mysterious author Simon mentions Manson's possible involvement with a nefarious secret society and places him in similar positions that Schreck seems to allude. The dots continue to connect in stranger and stranger ways.

At the beginning of this chapter I called these events one of the strangest cases in criminal history. I have proposed a few events where Manson and members of the family have been near influential people at random times. There is quite a bit of superstition and paranoia involved in the next chapter.

Manson appears in a few places during significant events seemingly unrelated to his known crimes. We are going to dig now. We are going to flip over some rocks and find fat squirming worms which are being devoured by ants. We are going to connect dots and try to put it all in one place. It is about to get weird.

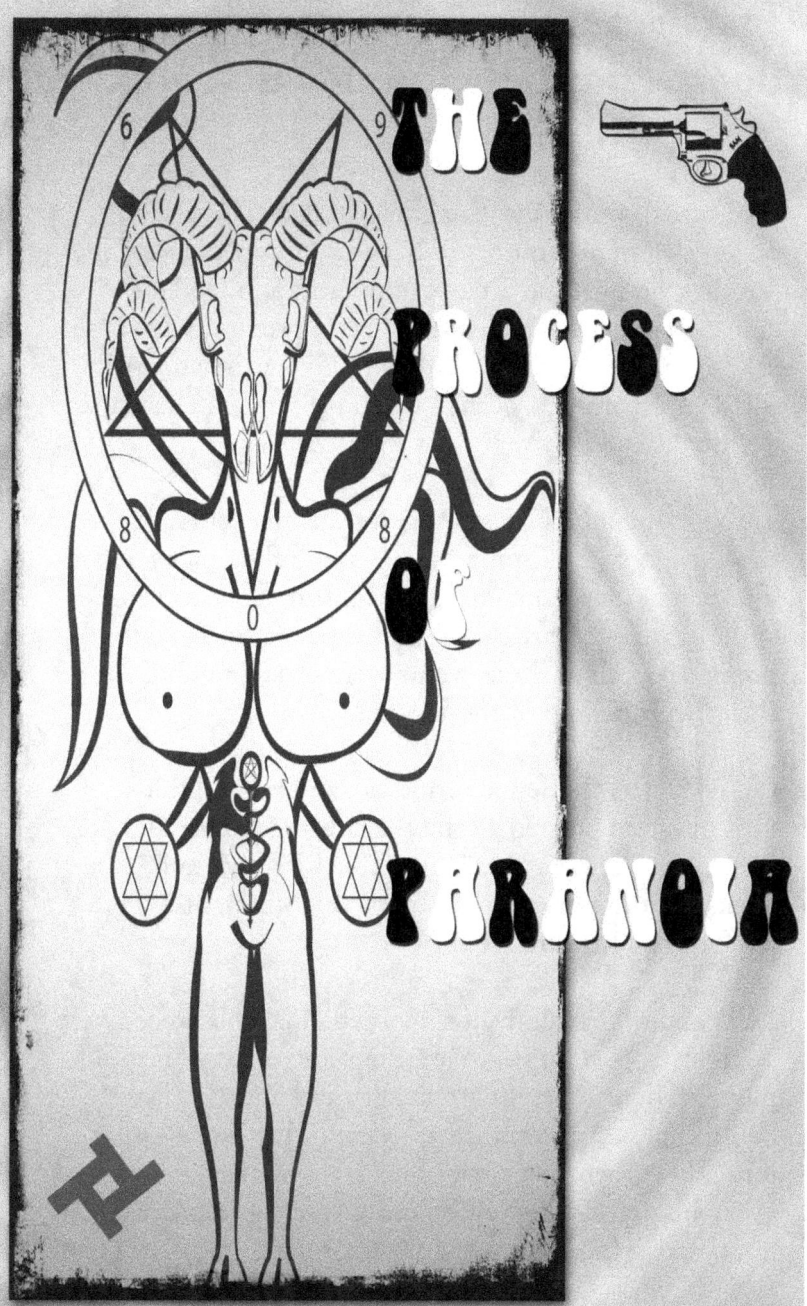

Just because you're paranoid, doesn't mean they're not after you. -Kurt Cobain

As I have promised we are going to take a bizarre turn on this leg of our journey. Charles Manson, some of the families victims, and a few of the most active Manson cult members have ended up in close proximity to some very strange events. The study will take us down a path filled with paranoia, occultism, conspiracy, witchcraft, and eventually murder.

Throughout the 60's Los Angeles was the center of the convergence of some unique and influential events. The events that transpired for Manson between 1967 and 1969 are of particular significance to what I am presenting. All of these events were occurring in front of the grim backdrop of the Vietnam war.

On 04/08/66, Time magazine asked: Is God Dead? This question created a tone that resounded throughout history. The era that Manson walked into when he was released from prison in 1967 was full of potential for a person with his skill sets.

LSD and other mind-altering medicinal substances were being used to raise your vibrations and open your mind man. Particular views on sexuality and androgyny were being explored and transformed into free expressions of love. There seemed to be a thick layer of clairvoyance over everything. Many were lost and wandering who desired guidance in these strange new territories.

People were breaking away from established norms and traditional values. Religious, cult, and occult organizations were working to become established on the East and West Coasts. Many of these groups found their footing, became deeply rooted and remain viable and active today. Some groups you may be familiar with are The Church of Scientology, The Process Church of the Final Judgment, and The Church of Satan.

Some speculate Manson was a member of The Process Church of The Final Judgment and another group known as The Children. The Process Church as it is commonly known is a splinter group of L Ron Hubbard's religious organization Scientology. The founder's of The Process Church of The Final Judgment were 2 former members of The Church of Scientology. Robert and Mary Ann DeGrimston. The pair became known as suppressive persons by The Church of Scientology. The DeGrimstons were both former auditors for Hubbard's organization.

Auditing is a process used by Scientologists to create a pathway to follow towards reaching the level of clear. According to Scientology clear is an individual who can be at cause knowingly and at will over mental matter, energy, space, and time. The DeGrimstons borrowed from Scientology and a new technique was born known as compulsion analysis. Eventually, compulsion analysis became known as The Process. The Process Church set up shop in an old mansion in London. The beginnings of The Process Church began in the basement of a coffee shop called Satan's Cave.

In 1966 shortly after setting up in London The Process Church moved to The Yucatan Peninsula to an undeveloped 4-mile tract of land. While The Process Church was in The Yucatan they developed the core structure of their philosophy. The Process is perceived as satanic due to some of their practices. The Process Church worships Jesus Christ and Satan. The idea is that at the end times Jesus and Satan will put aside their differences. Jesus and Satan will co-judge humanity. Jesus will pass the judgment and Satan will execute the punishment.

The Processes cosmology offers a few paths toward enlightenment. The Process provides 4 co-equal entities to choose.

Jesus Christ
Jehovah
Lucifer
Satan

Each entity offers a different path. Choosing the right path for you is based on your desire and your true nature. The Process has 3 main groups. The Luciferians who are pleasure oriented and hedonistic. The Jehovans who are staunch, rigid, and pious. The Satanist are rather mean, hostile, and violent. It did not matter what branch you belonged to because it was all going to be 1 and the same in the end The Process set up shop in San Francisco in 1967. When they landed in California, The Process Church members were often found ranting about the end times and doom speaking. The members spoke out on street corners or anywhere they could talk about the end of days and the times of trials and tribulations.

At this point a tangled tapestry is beginning to weave itself. These tenebrous lines connect and ensnare quite a few nouns. Here is a list I have prepared.

The Process Church
Scientology
Charles Manson
Anton Lavey
Sharon Tate
Roman Polanski
Mia Farrow
Robert Kennedy
The Beatles
Sirhan Sirhan
The Children
David Berkowitz
The Dakota Apartment Building
Simon
Marilyn Monroe

In 1967 Anton Lavey was a larger than life figure in San Francisco. Lavey's influence was felt all over the world but the original HQ for The Church of Satan was in San Francisco. The Black House as the church became known was a stark reminder of another side of the coin. Anton Lavey had created a new religion. Satanism is still a controversial subject. Lavey wrote The Satanic Bible and that was supposed to be enough of an explanation for his philosophy. Of course, many people never thought to look into the literature. Lavey and the black house seemed to be doing well at this point. Lavey had attracted the attention and membership of more than a few influential people. Considering the prominence Lavey had achieved it is not surprising that The Process Church reached out to him shortly after they arrived in San Francisco.

Lavey not being much of a joiner of groups declined their invitation to join forces. The Satanism Lavey established is not a theistic religion overall. Plus I am sure he probably thought they were a bunch of dangerous nut jobs. Lavey's proximity to the Tate Murders did not end here. It becomes apparent that Anton Lavey, The Process Church, and Charles Manson used Hollywood as a vehicle to perpetuate their very separate agendas to gain notoriety. They managed to get access to a lot of the same people around the same time causing all of these lines to converge into a very bizarre sequence of events.

In 1968 Anton Lavey played the role of the devil in the legendary horror film by Roman Polanski: Rosemary's Baby. If you have not seen this movie, you definitely should. The film was shot in The Dakota Apartment Building. John Lennon met his demise here at the hands of Mark David Chapman. Roman Polanski was the husband of actress Sharon Tate. Sharon Tate was not the only victim of these murders who had a relationship with The Church of Satan.

Jay Sebring had attended meetings at The Church of Satan's Los Angeles location roughly a year before he was brutally murdered alongside Sharon Tate by a group of Manson family members which included Susan Atkins. It appears that Sebring attended the meeting around the time that Sammy Davis Jr. was also attending meetings at the black house. What's that you say? Sammy Davis Jr. attended meetings at Lavey's satanic headquarters? Yes, he did indeed.

Davis Jr was a prominent member of The Church of Satan. Sammy Davis. Jr appeared to be relatively open about his involvement with the church. The late sixties were quite an original time. Being part of The Church of Satan became a kind of trend. Lavey realized this. The Church of Satan is interested in people who are productive, functional, and individualistic. Cult, mob, and herd mentality thinking, are not the traits of the type of individuals the church is interested in joining. I do not have permission to speak with authority on Lavey's philosophy. These are just my observations.

A more commonly known tidbit is that Susan Atkins played the role of a vampire in one of Lavey's productions. As strange as it seems, Atkins brief involvement with Lavey caused The Church of Satan to lose a chance to become more widely embraced. Considering that more than a few people still believe The Church of Satan is up to some insidious business. The 1969 murders unjustly verified the fears of the churches detractors. The murders were a direct attack on Hollywood and Lavey had worked to establish relations with some influential figures in Hollywood. Now that it was not just cool parties, orgies, and intellectual decompression. Satanism did not feel safe for them anymore. Susan Atkins passed briefly through the black house but did quite a bit of damage by association. Lavey also worked on a few other films. Lavey worked on a movie with another family member, Bobby Beausoleil. Bobby had a special arrangement with Kenneth Anger. Anger was associated with Lavey through the occult scene. The film was called Lucifer Rising.

Kenneth Anger created a unique film that is remarkable in its own way. It seems Beausoleil did not find Lavey's temperament agreeable and they did not get along well. About 2 years later Beausoleil murdered Gary Hinman. Jimmy Paige also was involved with Lucifer Rising. Beausoleil created the original soundtrack. Eventually Paige stepped in and created a soundtrack that was never used for the film. Paige released the soundtrack on vinyl in 2012. You can buy it on his web page.

There is a lot of speculation with the level of involvement that Manson family members had with The Church of Satan. Some people seem to think that Watson, Atkins, and a few other members of the Manson family were working on an offshoot of The Church of Satan. That is an interesting idea, but not viable in my mind. From what I understand The Church of Satan is not a cult or a community outreach program. There is a rigorous application process, and a hefty fee to boot for even being considered for membership. A screening process allows the church to decline membership to those that they feel are dangerous or unstable.

More than a few people have been miffed concerning their rejection by The Church of Satan. Sometimes these people decide to make their own brand of Satanism and declare themselves the black popes of their insecurities. I am not a member of The Church of Satan and I have never applied. Honestly it seems like Anton Lavey would not have wanted much to do with these guys or maybe even me.

Manson's involvement with The Process Church had begun before he was released from prison in 1966. Manson had been studying Scientology and claimed to have reached the level of CLEAR. In 1967 the Manson family was living on Cole street. Oddly enough The Process Church had moved into a beautiful property in The Haight Ashbury district a little further up the road from Manson. Manson was seen at the property often. As a story a goes, Manson reached the 4th level title of The Process Church. After being deemed a prophet, Manson was rewarded with a group to lead: Satan's Slaves. Satan's slaves got up to their own brand of murder, mystery, and mayhem.

Manson's general philosophy and his overall concern of Armageddon ran parallel to The Process Church and their view. Manson convinced his followers that he was both god and the devil. Instead of choosing one path to follow Manson seemed to reduce The Process Church philosophy to a simple duality. Manson became god and the devil to his followers. Manson also referred to his followers as the family. The Process Church referred to their members as the family as well.

As far as I can see it seems Manson's involvement with The Process Church ended shortly after the Tate/Labianca murders. Vincent Bugliosi writes about the 2 people who showed up to speak with Manson while he was incarcerated. Manson had been going on and on about his prowess, and involvement with The Process Church. As soon as these gentlemen showed up and spoke with him directly, Manson stopped claiming his relationship with The Process Church.

This event makes me think of the possibility that perhaps Manson was not involved with The Process Church. It could very well be that the accounts of Manson's involvement with The Process Church are lies or exaggerated. Maybe they saw Manson as a nuisance much like Lavey could have seen the family as a bunch of shit disturbers. Maybe these guys came down on Manson to convince him to stop speaking about his involvement with their organization.

What happened to Manson to make him button up like that? Manson has a reputation for being uncontrollable and defiant. Whatever it was it was enough. The Process Churche's involvement with Charles Manson is not the only thing that puts them under suspicion for other even more nefarious deeds. What I am going to do is introduce a few new characters into this conspiracy.

All of my research has always pointed to there being more than what is apparent. Manson is not the focus of the Tate murders. Sharon Tate and the people who were killed along with her are. My question has always been why? I have never seen these events as something random. There are too many variables involved. To end this paranoid diatribe we are going back to what I believe is the beginning of the madness. The next person involved after the birth of Manson on 11/13/34. Our timeline will start with the birth of a star.

DIAMONDS ARE A GIRL'S BEST FRIEND

Norma Jean Baker was born on 06/02/1926. The life that filled up the space of her short timeline is impressive. Before Norma Jean had her grand transformation she had a difficult life. I am not saying that things got much easier for her later on. She was young during World War 2. It was after the second World War that Norma Jean was discovered. In 1946 with just a little exposure Norma grew to gargantuan proportions. After her first screen test in 1946, the deal was sealed, and Marilyn Monroe was born.

After a few marriages stereotyped roles in Hollywood and growing weary of shitty contracts. Marilyn Monroe created her own production company and studio. Monroe became an archetype of feminine empowerment. Monroe was a gorgeous and complicated woman but she can also be remembered as being so much more than that. After her role in The Misfits and her last divorce from Arthur Miller Monroe succumbed to an emotional breakdown. After leaving the clinic she tried to get back at it,but she was fired from the last film she worked. At a short point after that she was found dead in her home of an apparent barbiturate overdose. On the surface it all makes sense. A Hollywood superstar who became the celebrated victim of her fame. The death of this megastar shook the foundations of Hollywood, the government, and organized crime.

Some heavy people would have loved for Monroe to meet an untimely end. The Kennedy's being some of the most notable. John Kennedy's affair with Marilyn Monroe was nowhere near as public as the affair that she had with Robert Kennedy. The infamous happy birthday Mr. President performance should be proof enough of that. Monroe's blatant extramarital enticement of Robert Kennedy was probably one of the nails driven into her coffin.

More information is discovered as time goes by that John Kennedy and Monroe were familiar with each other for a long time. The affair between them was very discreet. At a point in his campaign, he had to distance himself from her to avoid damage to his reputation. John Kennedy sent his brother Robert to kiss her off. The affair between Robert Kennedy and Monroe was instantaneous. Robert's lust for Marilyn and her ability to manipulate that desire made a pretty big mess out of things.

It is no secret that connection between the Kennedy's and Monroe is a possible factor of what lead to her untimely demise. Suspicion and proof that Monroe aka Norma Jean was involved in pornography and possibly prostitution keeps surfacing. Back in 2011 a short porn film was auctioned off for around half a million dollareedonuts. The film seems to have been shot between 1944 and 46. Norma Jean was discovered and was reborn. Kennedy being a hotshot politician probably had access to all sorts of extracurricular activities. Kennedy's links to organized crime are no more a secret than Monroe's.

Rather Monroe's connection to organized crime was a result of Hollywood, the Kennedy's, her own devices, or Frank Sinatra is not essential. When everything caught up with her she was already in between a rock and a hard place. Sinatra and Monroe were involved for some time and seemed to be very close friends. Sinatra felt like he could save Monroe from herself towards the end but Monroe seemed not to be so sure of this.

Monroe also partied with The Rat Pack whose infamous members included Dean Martin and Sammy Davis Jr. The possible long-term connection between Sammy Davis Jr. and Monroe could explain the relationship that Anton Lavey is believed to have had with Norma Jean. One way or another it is a very strange synchronicity. Lavey seems to have had a hot and lusty short-lived but significant relationship with Norma Jean. Lavey appeared to have had a thing for blonds.

Lavey was a real world class musician who had no trouble finding work playing the organ in tent burlesque revivals, carnivals, and strip clubs. Monroe was on the career path to acting and modeling that puts a young beautiful starlit in line with dancing and photo gigs. In any case, Lavey was at least a huge fan of Monroe and had no hang-ups about throwing a bad curse at those who would cross him. Things have not ended well for The Kennedy's.

New books and information are being released about the murder of Monroe. Claims are out there that she did not die until after she was discovered by paramedics. Researchers believe that the coups De grace was delivered and not accidental. Dead women tell no tales.

None of that changes that fact she is dead but it is important to know why and how. If the implications of all this are true it will change history and many skeletons would be revealed. A little over a year later John F. Kennedy was assassinated on 11/22/63. Other than the introduction of Sammy Davis Jr., Robert Kennedy, and possibly Anton Lavey. Frank Sinatra is added to our ever-growing roster. Sinatra married Mia Farrow when she was 21 years old in 1966. A soul-crushing 2 years passed, and things did not end up ideal for Farrow. Sinatra and Farrow clashed wills often, and Farrow eventually left. Sinatra was accustomed to a more submissive partner. They stayed friends.

All of them Witches

The divorce papers were served to Farrow on the set of Rosemary's Baby. After her marriage to Sinatra Farrow was looking for some direction and clarity in her life. Farrow eventually became interested in Eastern philosophy after visiting her sister and seeing the Maharishi speak. Mia learned as much as she could about meditation and ended up moving to India to study with her sister Prudence and the Maharishi. Another strange turn is the connection made in India with The Beatles. The Beatles had also come to India to study with the Maharishi as well. This chapter in all of their lives ended on an awkward note. Everyone returned a little disillusioned. Farrow was involved with Roman Polanski, Frank Sinatra, and Anton Lavey during the filming of Rosemary's Baby. Some bizarre things were going down in the Hollywood Hills. Before Sharon Tate and Roman Polanski moved into the Cielo drive property they were living in the rental property owned by Patty Duke. Tate and Polanski were prone to entertaining, and throwing parties.

It was during one of these parties that things got weird for Roman Polanski. Patty Duke's dog escaped from the yard. In the pursuit of Duke's sheepdog, Polanski was assailed by what came to be known later in a lawsuit as German Shepherds that were owned by the DeGrimstons, who were English occultists. According to the tale Polanski had to escape a garage he somehow became trapped in while being chased by The Process's cultist dogs. Barely a year later Tate and her friends were murdered on Cielo drive.

Sharon Tate had a significant level of charisma. Most people who encountered her became her friend in 1 way or another. On the set of Rosemary's Baby, FarrowTate, and Polanski became great friends. Roman and Sharon were very supportive of Farrow during her divorce with Sinatra. Sharon Tate was known for doing her own stunt work in her films. Eventually Bruce Lee became her trainer and stunt coordinator. Bruce Lee visited Tate and Polanski at the house they rented from Patty Duke. Tate's friends were far and wide. Sharon was also involved in politics and had taken a serious interest in the Robert Kennedy campaign. Tate and Polanski attended fundraising events for Kennedy. At one special fundraising dinner on 06/03/1968 at John Frankenheimer's house. Tate and Polanski were able to spend some time with Kennedy. Of course, being huge supporters of Kennedy they were thrilled. The next night Kennedy was shot 3 times by Sirhan Sirhan at the Ambassador Hotel after Kennedy had won the California presidential primary.

Sirhan has been linked to The Process Church as a devotee. Sirhan was also connected to Tate and Polanski through their social circle. After briefly establishing a headquarters in Los Angeles The Process Church more or less dropped out of sight the day after the Robert Kennedy assassination. Sirhan was known for his interest in The Theosophical Society and other occult studies. Sirhan has often been considered a type of mind-controlled patsy. It does not help that a member of The Process Church worked in the kitchen of The Ambassador Hotel and was a friend of Sirhan. Sirhan was also seen with a trio of people before the assassination. Most notoriously a strange women in a polka dot dress. At this point minds are most certainly blown and the wheel keeps spinning.

While all of this was going on Manson was a very busy bee. One of the things that kept the family going was relentless recruiting, and spreading the word of Charlie. A month before the Robert Kennedy assassination Manson sent some of his best and brightest to Mendocino county in Bonneville California after taking a rather circuitous route one destination being the Haight Ashbury free clinic. With all of the free love going on The Haight Ashbury Clinic was working overtime birthing babies and pumping hippies full of antibiotics. The free love movement also created a rash of children, and an epidemic of venereal disease. Abigail Folger's mother was a great supporter of the free clinic and helped raise quite a bit of money for the hospital. As it turns out Tate, Folger, Manson, and other family members attended these events at the same time. After getting treated for VD the family arrives in Bonneville in an old battered school bus. Reeking of patchouli, asshole, and their indiscreet drug use. The girls quickly drew attention to themselves. The locals referred to them as The Witches of Mendocino. Mary Brunner, Susan Atkins, Patricia Krenwinkel, and Ella Jo Bailey were a notorious coven in their rights.

The girls made the mistake of feeding a 17-year-old local LSD. The boy's mother found her son babbling about his hallucinations, and the boy told his mother that the Manson's girls had given him the LSD. A raid of the property where they were crashing took place. The girls were arrested on 06/22/1968. A few months later, on 10/14/68 a triple homicide, that mirrored the Tate murders occurred in Ukiah California. Some of the Manson family members were crashing in the area at the time of the killings while they waited for their court cases to settle up over the Mendocino drug bust. Manson had visited the girls while they were being held in Mendocino.

On the morning of 10/14/1968, Clyda Dulaney' son, discovered both his mother's and his grandmother's lifeless brutalized bodies. Clyda was 8 months pregnant at the time of her tragic death. The unborn baby is the 3rd victim of this horrendous event. Clyda's husband was Patrolman Don Delany. Don had supposedly arrested a group of Manson's disciples who were tripping on acid while driving with a baby in their vehicle. Some believe the family members got officer Don's name and committed this act of revenge on Don's young wife for having a hand in one of Manson's babies being put into foster care. Once Sheriff Bartolomei heard of the Tate murders he recognized a pattern and Manson's name due to the shameless self-promotion of The Mendocino Witches. The sheriff reached out to the Los Angeles PD to get photos and prints of the family members involved in the Tate murders. Nothing ever came of it and the murders are still unsolved. Today the Ukiah murders are considered by some to be the foreshadowing of the Tate murders. The savage brutality is an obvious connection. The women were bludgeoned and strangled to death. The Manson family, Don Delaney, and a few transient men have been suspected of the murders.

While I was researching this aspect of the Manson family conspiracies I realized something. Mendocino County has a violent history of its own. One of the first articles I found concerning Mendocino county was about a recent gunfight which had gone down between a wanted murderer and a local business owner. The business owner caught a guy pissing behind his business. The business owner gives him the what for and thinks it is over. The man comes into the shop with a double barrel shotgun. The business owner attacks him with a collapsible baton and knocks the gun out of his hands.

The crazed pisser manages to get the shotgun back and tries to blast the shop owner who ducks into the back room for his pistol. At this point shotgun gun dude cuts out and the shop owner takes a few shots at the stolen BMW as the pisser flees for the hills. More news show other homicides, bodies found, missing people, and more than a few unsolved murders. Sadly meth has taken hold of the area as well, making everything even stranger. I even found an article about an old lady who was killed by a tree which fell on her house after numerous attempts at getting her landlord to remove the old tree. It seems Mendocino County, and the surrounding area is known for its own brand of murder, mystery, and mayhem. It is not unlikely the Ukiah murders were independent of Manson's designs.

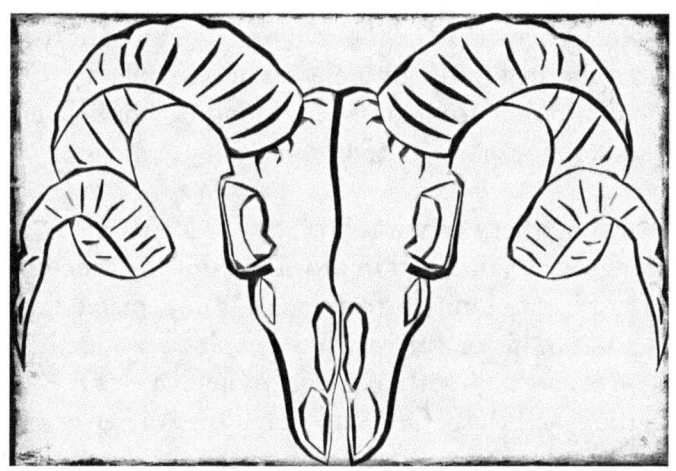

Fear of A Black Planet

Even with out all of things that could have happened. There are the things that did happen. The end time race war that Manson pitched was in line with The Process Church and their philosophy. Manson certainly seemed to be convinced that black people would have a revolution and take the power back from whitey. The contention between white people and black people runs deep. I can not wrap my mind around racism but none the less it is a reality.

It has always been easy for fearful fools to be incited to violence concerning xenophobia and the promise of the mob mentality. Manson and many of the occult movements in Los Angeles were also not very culturally adaptable. Other than The Church of Satan most of the groups in the area were not inclusive of black people. Of course all of these race issues are horrendous but for our purposes let's focus on 10/15/1966.

The Black Panther Party was born in California. Its beginnings were grounded in providing much-needed support and community protection. It is undeniable that at this point in history racist white people occasionally attacked, black neighborhoods lone individuals, and small groups of blacks. Of course, I am sure the favor was returned from time to time. The need for community support and a show of force was an inevitable response to the real danger black people were facing and still face today.

Of course white people responded in the same way. The fear is what drives racism. There were showdowns and armed public displays. Ultimately I am not sure if any of this made anyone feel safer one way or the other. Manson caught on to this and saw it as proof of the revolution. The only funny thing about this is that it was Manson's paranoia, which might have done him in. The Tate/Labianca murders and the murder of Gary Hinman were used as a way to frame The Black Panther Party for the killings. All of this started with a weed deal gone South between Tex Watson and Bernard Crowe.

After ripping Crow off for about 2,500 dollareedoos, Crowe reached out to Manson at the Spahn ranch. Crow told Manson that he was going to come down there, with some of his people and kill everyone. Crowe allegedly told Manson that he was a Black Panther. It seems that Crowe may not have been a member of the BBP. Crowe was shot by Manson in his apartment. Around the same time that Crowe was shot a BBP member's body was discovered. The word got back to the family and they associated that death with Bernard Crowe. Manson was not happy about attracting the attention of the BBP. Crowe survived the gunshot wound but was not in a great position to go to the authorities so he kept quiet. A short time after the Crowe shooting members of the family tortured and killed Gary Hinman. Hinman became associated with the family through Terry Melcher and other music connections Manson ended up sharing with Hinman. The family busted into his house and demanded he relinquish his property to Manson. There was a rumor of a large inheritance that Hinman had been rewarded that was not exactly accurate. Hinman was stabbed in the chest, beaten, cut, and had his ear chopped off by Manson before he was finally killed on 08/06/1969.

In response to the paranoia inspired by the Crowe shooting the family left BBP political propaganda behind at the scene. The messages were the panther paw print and the words political piggy, written in blood around Hinman's door frame. Only 3 days later similar cryptic messages were left behind at Sharon Tate's house written in her blood. Directly after that the same words were found again at the Labianca house written in their blood. The next step after helter skelter was for the family to escape into the desert to the pit. Here they would wait out the apocalypse. Ah yes, a grand utopia full of smelly hippies on dune buggies. Now of course there a are few holes in this plan. In the end according to the ideals that Manson put forth black people would eventually realize that they did not have the cognitive capacity to lead themselves. You know because Manson certainly was firing on all cylinders. At the point that black people have this realization apparently all at the same time they would turn to Manson to be their leader basically because they had murdered all other white people by the time they come to this realization. I mean Manson would be the obvious choice right!? No, he would not. We at Mad Robot and A Bizarre Compendium, despise all fascist, racist, terror-driven, groups, cults, movements, and individuals. Our collective feels these ideas of supremacy and segregation in all cultures are the biggest things holding back the human species. Imagine a world where we have moved past this bullshit. .

Uroboros

The Tate massacre could just be a random series of murders. Things could just be as they are. The established truths are bad enough without adding all of this other madness. The lives of all of the people who I have presented here are full of tragedy. The lifestyles of celebrities are often filled with all of the amenities that their fortune and influence can acquire.

All manner of magician and charismatic cult leader or Svengali have enticed otherwise jaded Hollywood royalty. The occult association with secret societies and private groups who offer an escape from the mundane are sought after by celebrity thrill seekers. Scientology is an excellent example of this. With enough money you can certainly move up the ranks of enlightenment. We all have our dark sides. At times our shadow self-needs to be fed. The 60's and 70's were another occult revival.

Sharon Tate was initiated into witchcraft while she was involved with the film Eye of The Devil. Being involved in occultism, parapsychology, and other out of the ordinary interests has never been the problem. Allowing yourself to be taken over by these practices is the problem. Keeping yourself grounded and avoiding guru worship is a good way to prevent some pitfalls.

It is easy to blame the murder on the gun, the knife, or the motive. It is not the devil that made someone do it. It is the person who let it happen, who lost control, who is responsible. It is each, who is accountable, for their own lives as they live them. Manson and others like him have decided that they like taking, they like crime, and they have discovered that it does pay and it is a quick fix in many cases.

Why not just take more than you need from whoever you can regardless of the cost to others? Why indeed? If we look at all of the murder that leads up to the Tate/Labianca killings we see a purpose for many of these deaths was to prove a point. And to exact revenge, or to perpetuate a hidden agenda that does not seem to have come to fruition. The implications of The Church of Scientology, The Process Church, and the shrouded group known as The Children are what help to make these tragedies even murkier

The serpent devours its tail a circle is complete. I am not the only one who believes all of these events and people are linked to an even greater conspiracy. The Church of Scientology, The Process Church, and even The Children are still operating today. The Church of Scientology is receiving some heavy scrutiny and much needed criticism lately. We are going to follow this timeline past the point and the events of 08/09/1969 too the East Coast, where another series of events seem to be related to The Children and David Berkowitz, AKA The Son of Sam.

Simon says

In 1974 Herman Slater published volume 1 issue 4
of earth religion news. The article was about how the
pagan and witchcraft community had finally stopped
arguing about whose Goddess had the biggest balls. In
the advent of modern witchcraft there has always been
some constipation concerning what path is valid or the
validity of your ancestry. Herman Slater is the legendary
occult shop owner and high priest. The Warlock Shop was
located in The Bronx and was always full of a variety of
people.

In 1974 after the witches had settled down. The people
who seemed to stick out the most at The Warlock Shop
were members of The Process Church and The Church of
Scientology. These individuals were not the garden variety
Wiccan or pagan occultist that frequented the shop.
Although it was not uncommon to see these persons in
the shop they had no apparent reason to be there. People
began to wonder about what they were up to.

1974 was a quite a year. Significant events took place
during this time. Patty Hearst was kidnapped and
programmed by the Symbionese liberation army. Ronald
DeFeo murdered his family in Amityville New York.
There was another killing that took place that was not
as highly publicized. In a church at Stanford University,
Arliss Perry was ritualistically murdered. Perry's body was
left in an alcove facing the main altar. The killer(s) left
a candle in between her breasts and one in her vagina.
Her pants had been placed over her body in a fashion
that resembled a unicursal hexagram. Perry was beaten,
strangled, and stabbed behind her left ear with an ice
pick.

The legendary and enigmatic occultist known as (Simon) was involved with Herman Slater and the Warlock Shop. Simon held classes at the shop and various other locations on the instruction and practice of ritual magic. Simon spent a good deal of time at The Warlock Shop. Once the Son of Sam murders began, Simon and other practitioners all over New York concluded that there was more than one Killer. Simon writes about this in detail in his book (Dead Names: The Dark History of The Necronomicon). It became apparent to the locals in the know that the Son of SAM cult was using The Warlock Shop as a place to find potential victims and recruits.

The local occultist became speculative about the Son of Sam killings because they understood a variety of occult calendars and what cult could be using them. The cult in question operated out of Brooklyn. The Son of Sam cult was related to the drug and sex trafficking that was rampant in New York at the time. Organized crime affiliates could have been driving The Son of Sam cult. The cult could be used as a way to prove a point to those not in the rackets good graces. Plus a cult that practices human sacrifice does need people to sacrifice. Organized crime and dead bodies pretty much go hand in hand. Just like drugs, money, and guns.

In Maury Terry's book (The Ultimate Evil) Terry expands on the ideas that a fringe satanic cult was involved with the Son of Sam killings. In The Ultimate Evil, Terry makes the associations between The Process Church, The Children, and the Son of Sam murders. Simon's account of the time is based on personal experience and real proximity to these events as they were unfolding.

Another strange aspect of this case is the German Shepherds found skinned between 1976 and 1977. Around Christmas of 1976 2 boys found 3 German Shepherds laying together in individual plastic bags. The kids were wandering around the area where Berkowitz's apartment and John Carr's house was. If you recall, Roman Polanski was chased and cornered by German Shepherds. The Process Church was known for keeping German Shepherds. True enough, German Shepherds are popular dogs, but come on!

The German Shepard tradition for The Process began in London. Each member at the time eventually had their own German Shepard familiar. After Robert Kennedy' assassination, the bodies of decapitated German Shepherds were found in Santa Cruz California. A member of one of The Process' splinter groups known as the Four Pi named Stanly Baker gave reports of human sacrifice as well. Baker also admitted to being a cannibal. Other witnesses came forward and told tales of the cult leader known as the Grand Chingon.

Charles Manson was known to be referred to as the Grand Chingon. Was Manson the shadow leader of this splinter of The Process? It certainly is a strange connection. It seems that the main concerns of the Four Pi revolved around the drinking and draining of blood. Human, animal, or otherwise. David Berkowitz becomes involved in this stick icky we, by his involvement with a man named Sam Carr. Some believe that both Carr and Berkowitz took part with The Children as well.

After Berkowitz was apprehended and he whispered all of his madness to his jailers and other inmates about his accomplices. Informants started producing some mangled bits that began to back up some of Berkowitz's claims. Ties between occult groups, pornography, and drug trafficking were being established. A particular informant named Vinny was fed some precise details concerning The Sam Cult and The Children.

Vinny's squealing revealed that the cult known as The Children operated out of Westchester New York. The Children had groups all over the country. One of the main hubs being in Los Angeles. The informant also stated that The Children in New York connected with another organization in the area. Vinny also verified Simon's theory that The Children used The Warlock Shop and The Magical Child Bookstore for recruitment and potential victims.

The worm turns profound and much is exposed. The Children and The SAM cult targeted college campuses as well. The information that came forward revealed a dark truth. The cult activity in the area was real and its tentacles reached even further than anyone expected. The supposed leader of The Children was believed to be a Mason, probably of high rank, but no one knew for sure. It seems that the head of The Children was a lawyer who also dealt in real estate, held an office in White Plains, and was also involved with politics. This man is the alleged mastermind behind the SAM Cult killings. The informants also relayed that some cops in Yonkers were involved along with quite a few other people with influence in the area. The arrest of Berkowitz did not close the SOS investigation.

John and Michael Carr were both friends and associates of Berkowitz. John Carr resided in North Dakota in the mid 70's. There is scattered proof that John Michael Carr had been friends with Berkowitz for an extended time. Berkowitz stated that Michael Carr took him to a party where he was involved in a "Satanic" ritual. Here seems to be the time Berkowitz became involved with The Children and maybe even the Sam cult. John and Michael Carr were the sons of Sam Carr. Surely the significance is not lost on you here. Sam Carr was the owner of the infamous black lab who was ordering Berkowitz to kill and was driving him to murder due to his constant barking.

The belief that Berkowitz did not act alone is widely accepted by a lot of the investigators involved in the case. Some of the murders and shooting just did not add up. Berkowitz told a tale of a network of people involved in each shooting. It is even alleged that a woman was involved as the shooter. This theory adds up because witnesses to the crimes put the killer in locations that they could not have been based on where they had been seen. There is no way Berkowitz could have traveled the distance in time to make the shot where the victims ended up being when the shooting occurred.

Maury Terry did a great job deciphering the notes left by The Son of Sam. Terry put together a reference for John Wheaties to John Carr whose nickname was Wheaties. The letters left behind and sent out by The Son of Sam were filled with clues that The Son of Sam was not acting alone. John Carr also visited New York often and was heavily involved in the cult scene in North Dakota. Berkowitz also spoke about meeting with The Sam cult at Untermyer Park.

Untermyer park started out as Greystone. When Samuel Untermyer took possession of the property he changed the name. Untermyer was a lawyer who was considered a civic leader. Untermyer Park is located in Yonkers and Westchester County, New York. The property was developed between 1900 and 1940. Untermyer Park is filled with classic Greek architecture including an amphitheater. After a period, Untermyer Park fell into disrepair. The Children were believed to be active in this area and used the park often. The animal sacrifice remains were often left out in the open with little to no regard.

John and Michael Carr both died horrible deaths while Berkowitz was in prison. The circumstances concerning their deaths are very sketchy at best. It seems that Berkowitz was right and all of his accomplices very well could have gotten theirs in the end. We know the Carr's did. How are we to tell if anyone else involved got theirs as well? Today Berkowitz has renamed himself The Son of Hope and is a full-blown, born again, servant of Christ. I guess if anyone needed it, Berkowitz might be the one. Funny how that works.

Maury Terry does an excellent job in his investigation of all of this insanity. Check out his book it is excellent. All of this started back with Marilyn Monroe, to Roman Polanski, and then to Charles Manson. Finally we end up here with The Son of Hope and a lot of question marks. This timeline from Hell stretches all of the way to the Death of John Lennon, in 1980 at The Dakota Apartments and that is where I stop following it. Let's pick it back up with the bizarre murder of Arlis Perry.

Arlis Perry: in the garden of peace.

Berkowitz was stewing in prison in 1979. The Son of Hope mailed a book to the local PD in Bismark North Dakota. The book was about witchcraft. Written across one of the pages was a chilling phrase. The message stated that Arlis Perry was hunted, stalked, and slain. Berkowitz advised that she was followed to California and Stanford University. Was Berkowitz for real? Was Arlis a victim of The Children or The Sam cult as well? We have established that John Carr was active in the North Dakota cult scene.

Arlis Perry was born in Linton North Dakota. Arlis was heavily involved as a youth minister and spent a lot of her time working on spreading the word of her lord and working on converting "Satanists" and drug addicts. At a tender age of 19 Arlis married her high school sweetheart Bruce Perry. A few short months later Arlis was murdered in the chapel at Stanford University. Arlis had stayed behind the first year that Bruce went off to school. At this time Arlis was living in Bismark North Dakota. Arlis had been spending a lot of time ministering to the people in the area. Arlis and another young girl who was never identified.

Arlis Perry and her unnamed friend crossed the river into Mandan, North Dakota where they were attempting to convert some local "Satanists" to Christianity. After Arlis moved to Stanford to be with her husband Bruce she became a receptionist at a law firm in Palo Alto California. One day shortly after Arlis started working at the law office she received a visitor. Anyone who noticed thought the visitor was Bruce Perry. As it turns out it was not Bruce.

There was a lengthy heated exchange between Arlis and the stranger. After which Arlis went back inside and got back to work. The next night Bruce and Arlis got into a bit of an argument over some innocuous bullshit. Bruce realized that Arlis seemed to be kind of restless. Bruce figured that Arlis might be upset because he had been so wrapped in his studies. Bruce felt like he was not spending enough time with her. Arlis said she wanted to send out some letters and that she was going to go out and mail them. Bruce thought this seemed kind of strange. Considering that it was Saturday night and the mail would not even be picked up until Monday.

Bruce decided to go with Arliss. That is when the fight ensued and Arlis broke away from Bruce. Arlis told him that she wanted to be alone and was heading to the chapel to pray over things. Bruce went home and Arlis headed off to the chapel. A young man matching the description of the person who visited Arlis at her job the day before followed her into the last place she ever went. The next morning Arlis was found murdered after a frantic Bruce had attempted to get the campus security to check out the chapel.

It seems that they made a few half-ass attempts at checking things out. They discovered much later that a door had been tampered with. It looked like someone had broken out of the chapel. The Sunday services were held outside of the chapel in defiance of the murder and later that day the chapel was reconsecrated. Sadly Arlis was buried in the graveyard of the church that she was married in barely 2 months after her wedding. This event rocked Stanford University.

There is speculation that Arlis knew her killer and that he was a part of the group of "Satanists" that Arlis had gone to Mandan to convert. The possibility exists that Arlis may have had some passing relationship or friendship with the would be killer. When Berkowitz was approached about the book and its cryptic message he assured the authorities that neither he nor John Carr had anything to do with the murder of Arlis. Berkowitz spun a tale of an elite occultist assassin known as Manson II.

Berkowitz told authorities that The Son of Sam branch in Bismark wanted Arlis dead, so they reached out to the main headquarters in Los Angeles where Manson II became involved. Berkowitz said that the murder of Arlis was the work of Manson II and a few people from Bismark. Also probably at least 1 person she was familiar with. What is the reason that Arlis was targeted? Who knows what went down when she went across the river to convert those cult members? Berkowitz also stated that Manson II helped establish the Manson family cult and was involved in the Son of Sam murders.

Berkowitz was throwing Manson II under the bus because he was convinced that it was Manson II who had chosen him to take the fall for the Sam murders. Berkowitz was made into a patsy by The Sam Cult. So Berkowitz was trying to turn evidence that could implicate others in the killing of Perry. During 1974 and 75 there was a surge in Manson family activity. Including the assassination attempt of Gerald Ford.

So here we are again. Berkowitz exposes the possibility that all of these events are connected in one way or another. By this time investigators are positive Berkowitz did not act alone. It seems that the local authorities did not have the resources to conduct an investigation that spanned between LA and North Dakota.

This timeline exposes decades of murder, mystery, and mayhem. In the 80's the satanic panic created a nation of fear. The ideas that were set forth were impossible. The amount of people being kidnapped was astounding. So astonishing that the claims could not be substantiated by evidence. The first wave of sensationalism passed, and quite a few peoples lives were ruined. The satanic panic died down. Of course, The Church of Satan was implicated in most of the activity, but it is doubtful that they were involved.

The brand of Satanism enforced by The Process, The Children, and The Sam Cult is very different than what Lavey established as a religion. It is undeniable that these factions exist. These events happened. I believe these claims and association simply because it is crazy enough to be true. Many restless dead, bloated flies and ghosts are surrounding all of this. Bodies disposed of never to be found. Dirty Deeds done in the dark and shadows. The ones that are meant to be seen are. For whatever the methods, the means, or the motive, it is certainly a bizarre world out there.

What is the last terrifying piece of this true tale of terror? Arlis Perry was murdered on Aleister Crowley's birthday. I don't know but this fact is more than a little disturbing. I contemplated not using this little tidbit. I realized that I would be going against the spirit of this anthology. Uncle Al's face is plastered all over the evidence folders of some of the most infamous true crime tales. Crowley was an amazing occultist among other things. The great beast made sure that he was the gold standard of occultism. It is true that Aleister Crowley was not a person you would choose to look after your pets. For the most part he was a kind of super villain. Much like Charles Manson, Crowley's bulging bug-eyed stare glared out at a different generation. Crowley had a significant influence in my life concerning occultism. I will leave this here for you to make up your own mind.

THE

OCCULT

(Occult) Everything from this point forward is heresy. The study and practice of occult sciences are the abandonment of willful ignorance, self-deceit, guilt, and blind faith. A quest to revealing secrets and hidden knowledge. The continuing practice of developing an understanding of the paranormal versus the measurable. The occult is a topic as varied as its practitioners and practices.

I will define an occultist as an individual who is concerned with their personal growth and development. A person who works to expand their achievable reality to become more aware of self and other. The measurable is meant to grow. In my life experience and world view, it has always been the occult vs. religion. All things outside of the doctrines and dogmas of your religion are not only ludicrous but forbidden.

Pagans, Indians, witches, and other people have all fallen to the blade of organized religion or are eventually crushed under the heel of those powers that be. Broken cultures, traditions, and civilizations ground into submission or extinction by the Abrahamic war chariot. Occultism, magic, and parapsychology lead directly to the realm outside of the kingdom of man, and its god. What is real? How is it real? Reality is often defined by consensus, politics, religion, or tradition.

So yes the line is drawn. The persecutors of magik and the occult seem to do their best at keeping the questions silenced while maintaining, and manufacturing all of the reassurance you can swallow. Occultism often removes a safety net that has kept us grounded. Performing a banishing ritual, casting a spell or sigil, is a direct act of free will. You are working to affect change without anyone's permission.

Now that you are past my pitch understand that there is danger involved. Insanity, isolation, obsession, paranoia, and even death has occurred in the pursuit of occult knowledge. Secrets are secrets for reasons. It is best not to be a dabbler. Either do it or don't. Occultism is not a halfway game. I know many people who just research, collect data, and study. They have a less practical interest in the occult.

There is a fear of the possible unknown consequences. For others there is just no belief and the occult is just an interesting topic. It is also forbidden to some people but they still study it to know the enemy. One thing I know is that most occultist have no problem with religion overall but that religious people have a problem with occultist.

There are more than a few occultist who have strong religious and spiritual faith. It is a good idea to have that in your arsenal as a magician. There is quite a bit of ritual magic associated with religion. So the line does blur. In my mind there is a significant advantage in being a cleric magi. The skill set allows for knowledge and the ability to use it.

Part of the fear is the practice. I think that is why an occultist has fewer problems with religion than the religious have with occultism. Many occultist come from a religious background so it is not a mystery. Instead of heeding the warning or embracing the fear I crack the grimoire open, create the seals, cast the spells, and study the forbidden. On the surface it seems like I am going to be ok spiritually but I guess I am just assuming this because I have not been struck down by lightning and plagued by demons or angels.

I feel I have communicated with deity, angelic, demonic intelligent spirits, and ghosts. I believe that I have talked with some things that are not so easily quantifiable. Through occultism and occult practice I have manifested thought forms, cast spells, and sigils that seem to have worked, and enhanced my life in some bizarre ways. Do I know?

Well yes, sometimes I do know for sure that my efforts are what caused the changes that have occurred. Honestly, I still have more questions than answers. In a way, blind faith carries an occultist as well. It is the self-assured confidence that comes with results. How does it work? I do not know I only can guess.

It is possible for me to tell theoretically how some of these techniques might work using a psychological model. Typically applied psychology, Jungian psychology, and other schools of mental discipline can be used to explain some magical practices and the results that occur due to those activities.

The Satanic magical model set forth by Anton Lavey has three aspects; lust, destruction, and sympathy. Each one of these techniques can be described as using hermetic magic. Hermetic magic is sometimes referred to as sympathetic magic. In the destruction ritual you would use an effigy or belonging of the person you wish to "destroy." The effigy acts as a representation of the subject. I know that this type of magic can be used to harm people or destroy them. I fully believe this.

Lavey also suggested "symbolically" destroying someone over wishing for their absolute destruction. At the same time, he did not seem to be opposed to the destruction of your enemies either as long as you mean it. By symbolically destroying your enemy you can knock them down a few pegs. Make them see the error of their ways in a matter that causes them public or private shaming or discrediting.

That is just how those guys do it. One thing that is similar to these techniques and others is the acting out. Even if nothing that you are ever aware of happens to someone who has harmed you in such a way that you would curse them and pray for their destruction. You still did something. The magical experience is intended to be cathartic. A release of energy the hatred, anger, and desire for vindication.

Whatever your intentions are they are actualized through ritual. You feel like you have done something. Sometimes that is enough or it gives you the boost and bonuses you need to get it done. Then there are the times that something happens. At this point some people turn back to religion.

Some go mad. Well, I guess we all go crazy when that happens. When something that you believed could not possibly happen, happens. The event has an impact on your sanity. Look at the physiological effects of trance, meditation, and both excitatory and inhibitory states of mind.

Even just closing our eyes helps increase our alpha brainwaves and change the way we perceive and process experience. Doing so could be considered a magical act in itself. We hear strange tales of yogis who slow their hearts down to a terrifically slow rate.

Not to mention the way people rave about the results of meditation and yoga. The results are tangible and verifiable. There is no wondering rather or not it is working. You only feel great. Magic is not just cool hats, waggling fingers, and arched eyebrows. In our worlds it should be easy to see just by looking around. There is so much more to it than we will ever know.

Take some time. Decide how you define magic and the occult yourself. See how many of these definitions change after you start practicing. You might feel differently after your first ritual. You might decide to hang it up. Find out how it works for you and expand on it. You will find my contact info in this book. If you have concerns get a hold of me. I would love to hear what you have to say.

The system and the procedures I am illustrating here are the organization of techniques that I have assembled to create a particular system of magic. The purpose of this system is to construct, charge, and launch sigils with the goal of liberating the true will.

Sigil magik is not my creation but the system I am sharing with you is a unique collection of borrowed, original, and customized know how. I was introduced to sigil magic by Phil Hine through his book Condensed Chaos. Like many people, Phil Hine was influenced by Austin Osman Spare in one way or another.

Spare was a great artist who made some very sizable contributions to occidental magic. Historically Spare was not interested in normal society or fame as a prolific artist. For a short time, both Crowley and Spare worked together. Spare broke away to develop his occult philosophy. In any case it was Kenneth Grant who kept Spare's ideas and shared them.

I have used sigil magic for the last 24 years, and I have had some interesting results. My seminal occult practices were very structured and jammed full of props, costumes, trappings, and traditional ceremonial magic procedures. Over time I decided that all that pomp and circumstance just was not practical all of the time. I needed more flexibility and spontaneity. I spent quite a bit of time in my life being transient. I rarely had a set location for ritual purposes.

I had set up some temporary altars and spaces in the forest, under bridges in small towns, in abandoned houses, and buildings, basically anywhere I could get some privacy. Occasionally depending on the types of rituals I was experimenting with, I would get other people involved as celebrants to participate in the ceremony. More often than not these people would have a space we could perform our ritual.

I wanted a way to quickly cast and prepare spells. I mean sometimes you will need something in a pinch and you do not have the time to wait for the waning moon to be in Aries. Or you may not even have an altar to prepare in the north or so on and so forth. Oddly enough right about here is where a local occultist that I had run into while staying in a small town in Indiana, gave me Phil Hines book Condensed Chaos.

The cat in question told me that he could not wrap his head around it and he thought it would be right up my alley. I took the book and basically devoured it, threw it back up, and ate it again. I was smitten. I automatically understood this system as something more akin to sorcery. I knew then that I was a Chaos Magician.

Understand that I value my magical experience, study, and practice. Even though sigil magik is not burdened with dogma or ritual: discipline, technical achievement, and understanding are necessary to achieve results. Chaos and sigil magik is not for the lazy and undisciplined who are only looking for shortcuts. Chaos magik is a very eclectic and of course chaotic approach to magik.

For me sigil magic is one of the best schools of the occult sciences available. If done correctly the approach is highly accurate to manifesting your will and intention. I will iterate this a few times in this section of this book. It takes more than magik to get the job done. Consider creating and casting sigils as an enhancement to a plan that you are putting into action.

I am of the mind that you can certainly pray for rain, but you should probably dig a well while your eyes are on the sky. Becoming a magician is a way to improve your life not to make you less functional. I use magik to "blur the techni-color" not as a cure-all to every situation in life. We must do our best to keep at least one foot rooted in "reality" at least some of the time.

Alrighty then!

Lets strap on our tin foil hats

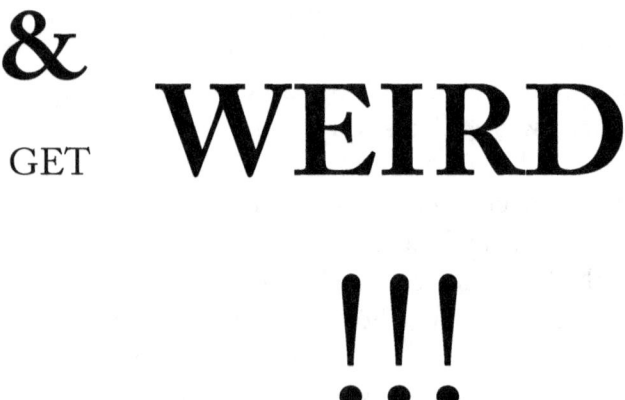

& GET **WEIScratchD**

This is a testimony to all I have seen, and all that I have learned...

- Abdul Alhazred

This is not quite a testimony to all I have seen but it is a little slice. The information that you are going to find in these pages is a lot like a loaded handgun. Sitting idly off in your periphery it is just taking up space. Maybe it is just an ominous paperweight but it is still there just full of possibility and implications.

In both the right and wrong hands this information can be used destructively and irresponsibly. At the same time just like using any tool your skill can be honed and refined. You can be a crack shot or you might end up shooting yourself in the foot or you might even blow somebodies head clean off.

So what is "this" information? Why does it matter? Why should you give a good (g)od damn? Hear me out. What the information is consists of the means and rudimentary knowledge it takes to set you on your path to using sigils and chaos magic. Just like anything worthwhile you have to do it. Give it a shot for no other reason than just saying you have done it.

Sigil magic can be very fun and practical not to mention a great creative outlet. Now, this information matters because you are looking for something. If you are here then you may have found it. If this is not quite what you were looking for keep searching.

In other maybe more recognizable terms, you could learn to create change in conformity with your will. Even if you have heard this before it still sounds pretty dark maybe even grand or vague. I will show you how to communicate with your unconscious mind by using a proto-language you design and customize. You will learn how to clarify, specify, and determine what it is you desire and how to manifest your will.

Seems pretty great right?! Hell yeah it does! So let's get to it. In one way or another we are programmed. We are prompted to receive commands, suggestions, and messages all of the time. We are influenced by both external and internal forces. Our internal dialogue, hopes, fears, beliefs, and emotions along with external influences like the media, societal, and cultural norms bombard us with a steady stream of sensory information all of the time. By becoming aware of this you can directly influence all of the nouns around you.

At the same time you can consciously choose a course of your evolution and actively work to manifest your true will. So if you are of the mind secret societies and the media are brainwashing you. Why don't you just brainwash and reprogram yourself how you see fit?

A sigil is a symbol and quite a bit more. A sigil is something that is constructed to have an esoteric meaning that contains a command to execute your will and manifest your desire. There is only a process. There is no particular way or set of symbols, beliefs, deities, or dogma, that is needed to practice this technique. Honestly, I think it is our responsibility to try to expand on these methods.

Sigil magic can be considered a very personal craft due to embedding your command deep within your unconscious mind. In the very back of your mind the intent, power, idea, or however you define it lays in wait simmering and getting ready to pop off.

During the process of determining your intent and creating your sigil. You must remove your lust for results and obscure the original intent and purpose of the spell by using a reduction process. The idea is to take a complex desire which has a lot of meaning to you and then reduce it to a statement of intent. By the end of your process the words that made up your desire are reconstructed into a symbol that is unique to your will and intention.

Yes I know it all sounds very sci-fi, but it works. There are just a few steps to follow and a few things to keep in mind. First 3 things, then what to do, and how to do it. So just hold tight or skip ahead to the pictures, charts, and diagrams.

1. Know yourself - Know what it is that you want. Sometimes in life we just start doing things to feel like we are making something happen or that we are working towards a goal. At times when we finish the journey and arrive at our destination we are not sure why we are there or how we got there. The results do not always match the intent. When we take action in life it is for a variable number of reasons. Why we do things is an interesting question. Why we want things is something else altogether. Our desire can blind and deceive us into wanting things that we do not need or truly want. When this happens we are more susceptible to our environments and our true will is compromised. At this point you could start living vicariously in an unhealthy fashion or just go along with what is expected of you while you ignore your own needs. Being in this type of state allows you to be influenced rather than shaping the worlds around you. Imagine how you feel when you truly need something in life versus just wanting it. At times it may feel like just getting what we need is hard enough and our hopes and dreams are just outside of our reach or light years away. Some people just totally give up and transform into amorphous clouds of wailing gas who are haunters of life and joy. The ever sullen full of skepticism and warnings.

In any case many magicians could agree that periods of self-assessment are necessary to filtering out all of the nonsense and getting to the results. Stepping back and taking a look at ourselves from time to time could save us a bit of trouble. Stopping, thinking, and taking a second to work it out is one of the best ways to come to a real conclusion and solution.

Make sure what you are doing and how you are doing it is conducive to your well-being and happiness. Of course, we can not always exist and live in ideal circumstances, but we can make things better any way we can. We just need to be adaptable. By being aware of our needs we will become more aware of how to fulfill them.

Get to know you periodically. You might be surprised by the person you meet. Our needs want and desires change over the course of our lives. Staying in touch with those parts of yourself is helpful. We can choose how we live and what we do with our time. As long as we live along the course of our true will. **Know yourself.**

2. Think it through- Make a plan. After you have decided what you want to figure out how you are going to get it done? Step 2 seems to point back to step 1. Another period of self-assessment could be used to determine your course of action. After all if you are doing the work make sure you know you can get it done. Make sure your plan is realistic based on your achievable reality. Do not set yourself up for failure.

Magic is not going to just happen on its own. You can not be a spectator in this sport. You have to be actively involved with your craft and develop an intimate relationship with yourself. By generally becoming more aware you can find the little esoteric Easter eggs that help make the impossible possible. One way to guide your course of action that is not uncommon among magicians is to use divination as a tool to help solidify a plan. You may also use divination to determine if and when action needs to be taken.

So in the process of constructing your sigils you could develop a relationship with a form of divination that suits you. If you take this route try a few methods. I like the tarot, I ching, and astrology. Find your own. Tea leaves, runes, reading entrails, there are more than a few ways to divine.

You could also try to talk it out with people. Bouncing the ideas you have off of people whose opinions you value can be beneficial. You still have to do what is right for you in the end. Talking it out just might help you get there.

You might even get helpful advice on how to go about gaining your desire through other means. Just saying it could set things into motion. We have to be active, pay attention, and be aware of our resources that are around us. We are always surrounded by possibility. We have to engage our lives to get the results we desire actively.

So if you want to lose weight you can not do this by watching exorcise videos, not eating fat cakes, and talking to people about losing weight. Ask yourself why? Why do you want to lose weight? How will losing weight change your life? How would you feel about living a more healthy lifestyle? What is a more acceptable level of fitness for you?

Describe your emotions concerning your weight loss and how you feel about yourself and how you think people view you. Determine the lines between self and other. Ask these questions and more. Write down a plan, see it on paper, so it becomes more real for you.

Plan for weight loss-
1. Determine a real start date for your endeavor.
2. Talk to a doctor to determine if your weight problem has to do with a physiological or psychological issue.
3. If #2 applies, seek treatment.
4. Set a target weight.
5. Talk to a dietitian and educate yourself about dieting and nutrition.
6. Change your eating habits and adhere to your diet plan.
7. Determine an efficient workout plan.
8. Join a weight loss and or an exercise group.
9. Establish a time frame that you want to lose a specific amount of weight.
10. Do not give up.
11. Once you achieve your goal, keep going until you are satisfied.
12. Keep up your discipline so it becomes easier over time and you do not have to repeat this process.

Of course this is just an example. You should create a plan that works for you. If by chance this example works for you feel free to use it. Ask yourself again in light of further consideration if what you are about to do is the best course of action? Ask yourself if you want your desire to manifest for this particular spell?

Consider how it could affect you and the other nouns in your life and the world as a whole. Is there a price and is it worth paying? Decide now, plot your course, and see it to the end. Have no regrets and take advantage of the things that using magik brings you. **Think it through**.

3. Do it - That's right damn it! I can't say it enough. You have to do it. Do the magic, make the sigil, cast it out, and do things that help increase the odds of your success. If you do not work out and stick to your diet plan, chances are nothing is going to happen. Magic is the result of your will. Casting the idea strengthens your likelihood of success.

You certainly can lose weight and get fit without sigil magic. Similarly if you wish to win the lottery and you do not buy a ticket or play your numbers your chances of winning the lottery are slimmer than ever. Casting for getting a promotion at your job could be pretty useless if you are doing terrible work. Going back again to #1 we might see that building a bright idea of who you are and what you want also plays a significant role in the success of your sigil magik.

Practice makes perfect. The more you do it, the better you get at it and the more you understand it. Becoming a magician and using these techniques require the development of technical excellence and discipline. Remember magic is a way of enhancing your life and a means to make things even more attractive. In the process we are going to have to learn some stuff.

Even though there is a lot of procedure and technique involved magic can be a lot of fun. Experiment with your sigils. Do something silly or weird. Cast a sigil to see a blue balloon at your workplace. Create a sigil to get a hug from a beautiful woman/dude. Try creating random scenarios that you manifest. Doing this will help you learn to recognize those ultra special magical moments that pop up in our lives.

Use sigils to have an impact on the more mundane aspects of your life. Get some practice and then build up to the big ones after you refine your techniques. Keep track of your results using your grimoire or journal. It is a good idea to keep a log book or magical diary to capture and record the grammar of your work.

These books of shadows can be great tools for self-assessment and mark the progress of your secret experiments. Chances are you may feel compelled to or have already created a journal. I mean everybody knows that sorcerers, wizards, witches, and all other kinds of impious blasphemers, have books of spells.

Do it. Before you do it make sure that you want to. Do not allow yourself to become dependent on these methods to solve all of your problems. Being a magician means that you are a competent, capable, skillful, and intelligent human being at the least.

How else are you to be expected to wield your true will if you can't balance your checkbook? It is effortless to get caught up in your work. Obsession and possibly unhealthy fixation with the occult can lead to some pretty negative side effects.

Keep in my mind these means will also lead you to some very positive change as well. So stay grounded. Step back sometimes and get a beer with your friend. Watch a buddy comedy instead of a documentary on Aleister Crowley. Spend a few days, weeks, or months not talking to everyone about magic. Sometimes getting back to the mundane from time to time is not a bad idea.

.

Know Yourself
Think it through
Do it

CRIM

The Nuts

Hopefully, you have made it this far. If you have thanks for hearing me out. If you have not, well then I guess you just are not going to know some pretty important secrets. What I am going to show you now is a simple procedure that will allow you to fabricate your sigil to the point of charging it and casting it away. One step at a time and in order of operations. It would be pointless to unload a gun and then dry fire it.

1. The motive of your desire - The first step is often referred to as your statement of intent. Here is where you decide what it is that you want and how you are going to phrase it. What is motivating you, what do you want, need, or desire? I emphasize it is important to have a well-planned statement of intent.

Do not use negatives or wishy-washy language. For Craig's sake don't be passive aggressive. Speak up and be heard. Make it clear.

I WILL WIN THE BINGO JACKPOT- Yes

I would like to meet a fun redhead sometime - No

I WISH TO GET A PROMOTION - Yes

Maybe I could do better on my final exam - No

I think you are picking up what I am putting down.

You might be trying to figure out how you can come to a clear statement of intent. This is sometimes easier said than done. You can go back to **#1, know yourself**. Define the problem or situation that is the source of your desire. What is the question you are trying to answer? For instance, let's say there is a bully at your job or school. Now come on, we all know that adults get bullied too. So listen...

1. The Problem =
A bully
2. Your Desire =
Freedom
Peace
Independence
Liberation
Revenge
Vindication
3. Your statement of intent =
A. *I will never be bullied again*
B. *I will find peace with my bully*
C. *I will reason with my bully*

The 3 different statements above all express a common problem. The bully. Each statement also offers a different approach to the problem.
A. Making a stand martially, with force, and possibly violence.
B. Using compassion, and empathy in an appeal towards peace.
C. Appealing to the logic and reason of the bully.

Magic insists that we think and live creatively. By coming up with 3 possible solutions I have taken some time to organize my thoughts about the problem and multiple approaches I can take to create the solution. Sometimes you can find a way to appeal to the heart and compassion of people. Approaching a situation in a rational manner and shining some light on logic and reason is always a great outcome.

Other times you might just have to smack someone silly because you can not appeal to their hearts because they are sociopaths. Good luck trying to use logic and reason on some people who are already mental and unhinged. Why not be ready and have a solution for all 3 scenarios. Drawing up a few statements can also help with the forgetting process that we will learn more about soon.

Approaching solutions in a creative fashion helps us become more capable and adaptable. We have all to often seen that when someone is pushed to the edge they lash out. Usually in a big way that may have some horrible ramifications. Sometimes when we lash out we become the monster and sometimes it feels terrific. That is why working past our initial anger, confusion, and fear that motivates us. When we are confronted is very important to come to a more productive less destructive solution. For our example we will use:

A. I will never be bullied again

2. Reduction/Reconstruction

A. Take your statement and remove all of the vowels.

I will never be bullied again - Before

w l l n v r b b l l d g n - After

B. Remove all double letters

w l l n v r b b l l d g n - Before

w l n v r b d g - After

C. A few options are presented with what is left.
1. Create a mantra
2. Reduce to a number
3. Recode in a new alphabet or symbol system
4. Skip to step 5
5. Create a monoglyph
6. Think of a different way all together
7. All of the above

C1- You can create a mantra with what is left of the letters. It does not have to make sense because you really do not have much to work with sometimes. Also changing the shape of the statement another step makes it easier to conceal the original meaning. In this case you might want to add vowels into your mantra, but keep them separated from the actual sigil.

w l n v r b d g - before

volg wrend - mantra

Do not forget to remove the vowels from your actual sigil. Do not include them in the monoglyph.

See what I did there? I broke the rules a bit to make it work. There is nothing that says that you have to remove all of the vowels to make this technique work. Doing so is my personal preference when creating a monoglyph. As long as you remove redundancies you are making it easier to lose your attachment to your desire and the result.

Mantras are helpful in charging the sigil. Chanting something over and over again in an excitatory state can get you worked up. You will need a build-up and release of energy to charge and cast your sigil. So consider it. Creating a mantra also further obscures your original statement.

VOLG WREND is total nonsense, but it sounds cool to me. It is also a very different thing than it started out as. VOLG WREND also sounds and feels magical to me on a personal level. It gives me a sense of martial power that fits the intention of the sigil. So chant it!

C2- You can use numerology to reduce what is left of your statement to a number. How you ask? I will show you. If you are unfamiliar with numerology, here is a quick break down as I practice the discipline. Each of the letters of the English language has a numerical equivalent with a range of **1** through **9**.

1	2	3	4	5	6	7	8	9
A	B	C	D	E	F	G	H	I
J	K	L	M	N	O	P	Q	R
S	T	U	V	W	X	Y	Z	

All you have to do now is look at the number and look straight down. All letters that equal the number **1** are **A, J,** and, **S** etc-etc-etc. If your name is Arthur then the number that represents your first name is, 1+9+2+8+3+9=32. So now we add the numbers 3+2 to reduce to a number ranging between 1 and 9, and we get 5. The number that represents the name Arthur is 5.

In our case VOLG WREND becomes 4+6+3+7+5+9+5+5+4= 43= 4+3= 7. Our statement of intent has been transformed into the number 7. Are you already starting to forget the original statement? Maybe now you can see why working the statement out makes it possible for us to remove our attachment to our desire.

C3- There are many alphabets to choose. Words letters and symbols are all sigils in one way or another. There are very alluring alphabets that are commonly used for magical purposes.

The Hebrew alphabet for one is a very traditional alphabet to use. Egyptian hieroglyphs are also quite the rage. Runes have quite a bit of magical potency considering they can be utilized specifically for divination. Of course the Enochian alphabet is also beautiful and made even more famous in modern pop culture by the show Supernatural.

I am sure you could find one that would suit you. You may already have done such a thing for some reason or another. You may be a super nerd and study the Elven alphabet from the LOTR series or even the Klingon alphabet. In any case both of these examples are appropriate. Once again the point is to remove your awareness of the original meaning of your statement.

I just make my own sometimes. You can too, and it is not as hard as you think. Being a graphic designer has helped me understand this process a little better. Spending time studying typefaces and font families has helped me learn to appreciate the subtle differences that contribute to making a character unique to itself and its group. Try creating a bit of sameness and style among your characters. Recognize that even though most typefaces and characters have many similarities most sets also have a few characters that are also unique.

For instance, the difference between the letter G and the letter X. G feels more organic to me than X. X is a lot sharper of a shape than G. Even though they possess similar qualities they are unique when looked at individually. In my alphabet, I use the letters G and Z to create that bit of organic posturing. The letter Z has always felt mystical to me, so I gave it a bit more character.

(See Pg. 156)

It might be hard for you to equate 26 characters to a new and unique symbol system. Just practice. Creating alphabets is a great creative exercise. Doing so adds a very custom feel to your magical work. Of course this is not always necessary. As I have said there are many to choose from if you decide to take this route. An excellent source for magical alphabets is the book The Magicians Companion, by Bill Whitcomb. Check it out. You may also feel free to use the alphabet of the bizarre if you like. That is why I have added it to this grimoire. When we use the alphabet of the bizarre to recode our statement, we get

V O L G W R E N D

Now we can take whats left and make a monoglyph.

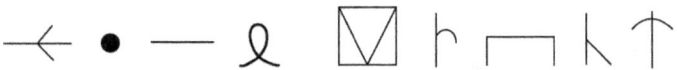

this-

C4- Skipping to step 5 is acceptable if you want to use the monoglyph method and do not want to use a different alphabet to recode your statement.

C5- What is a monograph? Let's take a look at the word. Mono as a noun is a combining form that means single or alone. Both the words glyph and mono are Greek in origin. The word glyph translates as a pictograph. A monoglyph becomes 1 symbol that represents many things. Just like your mantra. The monoglyph is the vehicle that you load your intention with to prepare it for delivery.

Typically I construct the monograph out of the letters that were left over from my original and reduced statement of intent. You can also use the number you have reduced your statement of intent to equate. You could also directly incorporate the number into the monoglyph. You could also include other symbols. I occasionally add planetary, astrological, alchemical, or even mathematical symbols into my sigils.

For this particular spell I would probably add the planetary symbol for Mars or Aries. Both of these symbols have a strong martial influence as archetypes, symbols, and deities. If you want that bully to fuck off you might want this little extra boost of Martian influence.

C6- Ultimately you do not have to do any of this. Take the little bit you have learned here, abandon my teachings, and blaze your trail. Expand on the already "established" notions on how to create sigils and wield sigil magik. Get excited and creative. Take all or some. Take what you want sprinkle it with your mojo, and get it done!

C7- Yes, that's right you can just do all of it. Why not? I mean it might help you feel like you have covered your bases. All of these methods work well together and separately. So mix it up a bit if you like.

The bolts.

#3 Design- The idea is in its form. Now that we have figured out what we want, how we want to say it, and the methods we are going to use to design our monoglyph. Let's make it real. The design step is my favorite part of the process. Here is where you will understand why the creation of a sigil is a rather personal and intimate craft.

Using the intention we have been working with I have created 2 monoglyphs. 1 is designed using the English alphabet it was originally written. The other is designed using the alphabet of the bizarre. I went ahead and added the vowels in the creation of the monoglyph. I know earlier I made a big stink about it. Sometimes we just have to be flexible.

The design process leads us back to **#2, think it through.** I enjoy being a designer, because when I work I enter an altered state of consciousness. When I am experiencing this altered state I feel relaxed, attentive, aware of my thoughts, and the overall significance of what I am designing is usually lost. Simply being creative can allow your entrance into an altered state of passive awareness and understanding. All you have to do is **#3, do it.**

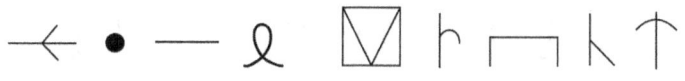

Even though I suggested removing the vowels from the monoglyph. I kept them in this design instead. Behold! Volg Wrend, the pacifier of bullies! As it turns out our monoglyph has adopted a rather martial presence. The sigil appears to be standing on a base. The stick-man quality of the symbol gives it a familiar humanoid form. Giving the glyph a familiar shape draws a sympathetic cord and a stronger affecting bond

You may keep the vowels in the monoglyph after all.

VOLG WREND

There are a few similarities between the bizarre and the English versions. The English Volg Wrend has a very, "Kick sand in your face" vibe to me. Both examples are humanoid in form and both display an aggressive confrontational deportment. I just put the characters together in a way that made sense to me. I read my interpretations of the glyph into the glyph. Giving it autonomy and alikeness in regards to the original statement while thinking and breathing life into it.

Simply done all that is needed is to fashion the leftover characters into the monoglyph. Build it to your specifications. Use whatever medium you can think to use. Paintings, carvings, pen to paper, digital imaging software, period blood, or some other way you can imagine. The digital age gives us more than a few exciting and innovative ways to design and launch sigils. Be creative. Get weird with it and have fun.

#4 Forget about it- You have to forget to remember to forget.? It probably seems strange that after putting so much work and thought into your sigil you are just supposed to forget about it. Well, try thinking about it this way. When you started this process, you were not even sure what you were doing.

At this point, you have found a solution, clarified your intentions, and reduced your will and desire to something completely different than it started out as. You have transformed your thoughts and desires into something tailor-made.

A Mantra - From point A to point B I defined my intentions. I am going to remove myself from my desire for my will to manifest. By doing this my sigil will be able to do its job unhindered by my lust for result. - If it helps just remember you have done something about what it is you were having trouble. I call this the check is in the mail tactic.

Simply draw up the monoglyph. Take you sigils and stash them somewhere. Give it about a week. Add the launching of sigils to your regular magikal work. Or if you are not in a direct need hide your sigil some place it may take you a while to find. Hide it in a book, a winter coat pocket, or at the bottom of your fish tank.

Launch it right away and see what happens. Some people like Phil Hine suggest swapping them with other people who practice sigil magic. At the time that you are designing the Sigil you are embedding the code or the monoglyph, mantra, number, or all of the above, into the back of your mind. So all that is left after the cooling off period is to recall the code and launch it out into the aether.

#5 Launch sequence-Much like the stalwart engineer in the bowls of The Starship Enterprise you have to give it all you've got! The time of liberation is near. At this point it is time to charge and launch your sigil. Over time I have created a few hundred sigils. It seems like most of the time I have used a combination of all of the techniques I have already gone over and the ones I am about to tell you about it.

I have found that using a particular launch sequence helps create a constant I feel is needed to make my magical work efficient. Anton Lavey refers to timing being of utmost importance to magic. I agree. With timing comes the point where an action is taken when certain variables are in place. Even though things may appear to be random they can still be captured in a controlled structure and procedure.

While I was initially learning enough about sigil magik to start to form my approach to the technique I often imagined the whole idea in a sci-fi futurist theme. When I am referring to the launch sequence I am referring to the part of the working that you cast the spell. For whatever reason, my mind equated the casting of sigils to a 3 2 1 count-down.

My daydream became pivotal in understanding and being able to apply sigil magik in my life in a more intimate and personalized fashion. Other chaos magicians may refer to casting sigils as launching them, but that does not matter because the approach that each chaos mage takes is probably unique to the individual. In any case my approach applies a 3 stage process before blast off.

1. Banish- The term clearing the air can be used here. Another important part of any successful magical endeavor is to put your mind in the right frame for magical work. There are more than a few ways to accomplish this. I use a banishing ritual known as the lesser banishing ritual of the pentagram. I use this ritual because I can easily exchange the archetypes that are utilized in this routine to customize my working even further.

There is a detailed explanation of the banishing ritual in the next section of this book; The paranormal. I put it there because it also falls under the heading of protection methods. Take a look at the procedure and you will see that it is a method of clearing a space, calling for the protection, assistance, and observation of the 4 archangels, and setting the mood for ritual.

Gasp! Gasp you say? Did I hear a gasp! Occultist calling upon the archangels for protection, guidance, and observation? To you, I say, indeed! The archangels are not bad entities to have in your corner. I mean if you are going to believe in all of this nonsense, then these guys are results-oriented and that is the whole mission statement, right?

Now look, if you are of the mind, you could use the structure of the banishing ritual and fill in the blanks. Use deities, demigods, cartoon characters, demons, rock stars, or whatever else = 4 archetypes. Before we go totally off the rails just check out the lesser banishing ritual of the pentagram in the next section. After you build a relationship with the ritual customize it.

I use this method because it makes me feel like something magical is about to happen. You might not need all of that. Going into a magical frame of mind could be as easy reading a poem, going for a walk, taking a bath, jumping up and down on a pogo stick?!

Anything that gets you out of your daily mucky muck thinking and into a creative space where strange things are more probable and believable. Sexual arousal near the point of climax is also a nice way to get your mind right. Not to mention the building of sexual energy and the anticipation of the release is very much the same thing as casting a spell in my opinion. So give it some thought. Try a few things. Find the methods that work the best for you.

2. Charge- Charging the sigil is probably the most crucial aspect of this technique. With out energy it will do nothing. Now is the time to unburden yourself of your desire and transfer it to the sigil. Jam that suckers full of your intention and will. Not to be redundant, but if you are already using sex to wake up your magical mind you may be halfway there or closer... Staring at your sigil may or may not be very sexually arousing.

The idea is to hold the image of your sigil in your mind as you work your way to sexual gratification while chanting your mantra, if applicable either alone or with partner(s). However you swing. Imagine the sigil as being filled with a glowing hot energy as your sexual arousal builds. It might help to imagine making sweet, hot, sticky, love to your sigil. If you are working with a partner imagine them as the sigil. Your partner as a participant could imagine themselves as being the sigil. Get weird with it. Use glow in the dark body paint and get a black light involved.

Object concentration and visualization may seem hard at first but just thinking about the sigil until you naturally start to visualize it is a good place to start. Object concentration can lead to some strange phenomena of its own. I am suggesting that you stare at your sigil until it burns itself into your mind.

To date myself I am from the age of Atari. Pong was a big fucking deal back in my day. I used to sit in front of the TV with 2 paddles and play by myself. I was a pretty big nerd and of course I thought this made me pretty rad. I guess I still feel the same about that. In any case I would play so long that long after I stopped I could still see the glowing white rectangles in my mind's eye.

It got to a point where I could visualize the tiny square pixel bouncing back and forth between the rectangles. So anytime I was bored and I needed a fix. I would just play in my mind through the use of visualization. Ultimately that did not stop me from wasting even more countless hours glued to that 8-inch black and white TV. No one believed me of course, but aha ha ha ha ha! Look at me now!?

Try it. Try sitting and starring unwaveringly for as long you can. You either start to recognize properties of the object you did not see before, objects begin to behave differently, and your mind or reality could start to play tricks on you.

You can recall your mothers face or a stop sign or a particular landmark quickly. Try to remember a detailed image of things you see all the time. Eventually you will do this with little to no effort. After some practice try to visualize individual objects, faces, or landscapes. You might be surprised how easy it has become.

When you are ready and you have put yourself in that magical frame of mind. I want you to find a comfortable place to relax your body. However you end up oriented affix you sigil in a position where you can see it. Gaze unwaveringly at your sigil. Be mindful of your breathing and allow your body to relax. You should be chanting your mantra if you have prepared one.

Imagine your breath filling the sigil with the energy it needs to blast off into the aether and execute your true will. Try to see it glowing, building, and filling up with power. Sometimes imagining it spinning helps. You might try shrinking and expanding it in time your with your breath. It will take a while not to blink, to sit still, and to monitor your breathing. Just do it. Keep it up.

By getting better at doing these simple things you are already doing magic. Because you expand what you are capable of achieving. However you get there in either excitatory or inhibitory vehicles keep the sigil in your mind until it is time to launch. There are more than a few options for charging your sigil these are the 2 I most commonly use. Try as many techniques as you can find or think to use.

3. Launch (destruction/preservation)- You may be ready to blast off at this point. If you decide to use sexual energy to charge your sigil wait until the time of your climax and then release at the same time visualize the sigil disintegrate, dissolve, or even just disappear.

Ideally you will want to ejaculate directly onto a likeness of your sigil. The same rules apply to women as well. Release, visualize and then mingle sexual fluids with the medium of your sigil. The method seems very primitive because it is. The primal aspects of this technique are what also gives the spell more power. Revel in your gratification and release. Howl with the wind! Free your self.

If you are using the visualization object concentration techniqu, when you can no longer stare at the sigil slam your eyes shut. You should be able to see the sigil behind your closed eyelids. Shout your mantra 1 last time and imagine the sigil once again transforming into a launched state. Launch sequence complete.

A- Destruction- In a final act of defiance against inaction you could destroy your sigil. I suggest using an elemental method. Examples include burning, tearing it up and flushing it down the toilet, tearing it up and throwing it out the window into a breeze, bury it somewhere like in a house plant or something. Shoot it with a shotgun if you can. That feels good, and it is fun to shoot shot guns. Of course your mean of destruction could also be your means of launching your sigil.

B- Preservation- Sometimes I like my sigils so much I keep them around. I only take them to the point of charging them and leave them in that state. This way I could simply do a quick launch at any time. Also I design some of my sigils to radiate energies, attributes, and commands.

Depending on their purposes it is better not to destroy them. I have sewn them into clothes, made t-shirts, posters, painted them on my walls, and have even had some tattooed on my body. Being exposed to the sigil for extended periods of time also helps to embed it into your unconscious mind.

Here it can grow and slowly manifest its purpose. Just because you may have destroyed your sigil in the last step does not mean you can not create a new likeness and keep it lying around somewhere. That is pretty much it for the process. All that is left is to tidy up and come back down to Gaia and get your feet on the ground.

6. Grounding- Last call. You don't have to go home, but you can't stay here. It is time to step out of that thrill of confusion and space cadet glow. The bouncers have kicked the lights up and everything just is not the same anymore. So kick mud. Hit the bricks. Get a gyro and some fries to soak up all of that magic in your mind and body. After any magical working it is good to tidy up.

Blow out your candles, open a window, say a prayer, jump in the shower. Do something to get your mind out of the magical trance and back into the 2nd bedroom of your 2 bedroom apartment or another dwelling or space you might inhabit. Take grounding literally and go out and stick your feet in the grass or dirt. Come down.

If you keep a grimoire make your notations and do your paperwork. Think about the ritual. What did you like? What did you not like? How did it make you feel? Did anything strange or unexpected happen while you were performing the rite? Record any dates, times, cycles, astrological events, or anything that you feel might have an impact on your spell casting.

So that is that. A quick and dirty rundown on how this works. Take it. Do something. Change your life. Use this information as a platform to jump off. I invite anyone who may practice these techniques to contact me directly and share your results and innovations. Before I wrap up this section. I am going to put in about 3 or 4 pages of some serious psycho babble revolving around brain waves and the differences, between beta, alpha, theta, and delta waves. I have even created a nifty infograph to make learning even easier. So fire up that doobie and pass puff pass. It is about to get heady. Hey, don't worry it is'nt going to be too bad. It is not like I am a rocket surgeon or something. I am just a guy who has dreams and does magic. Somehow both work and I am just curious about why and how. So I look into it. Prepare yourself and get ready to go.

BEYOND THE WALL OF SLEEP!

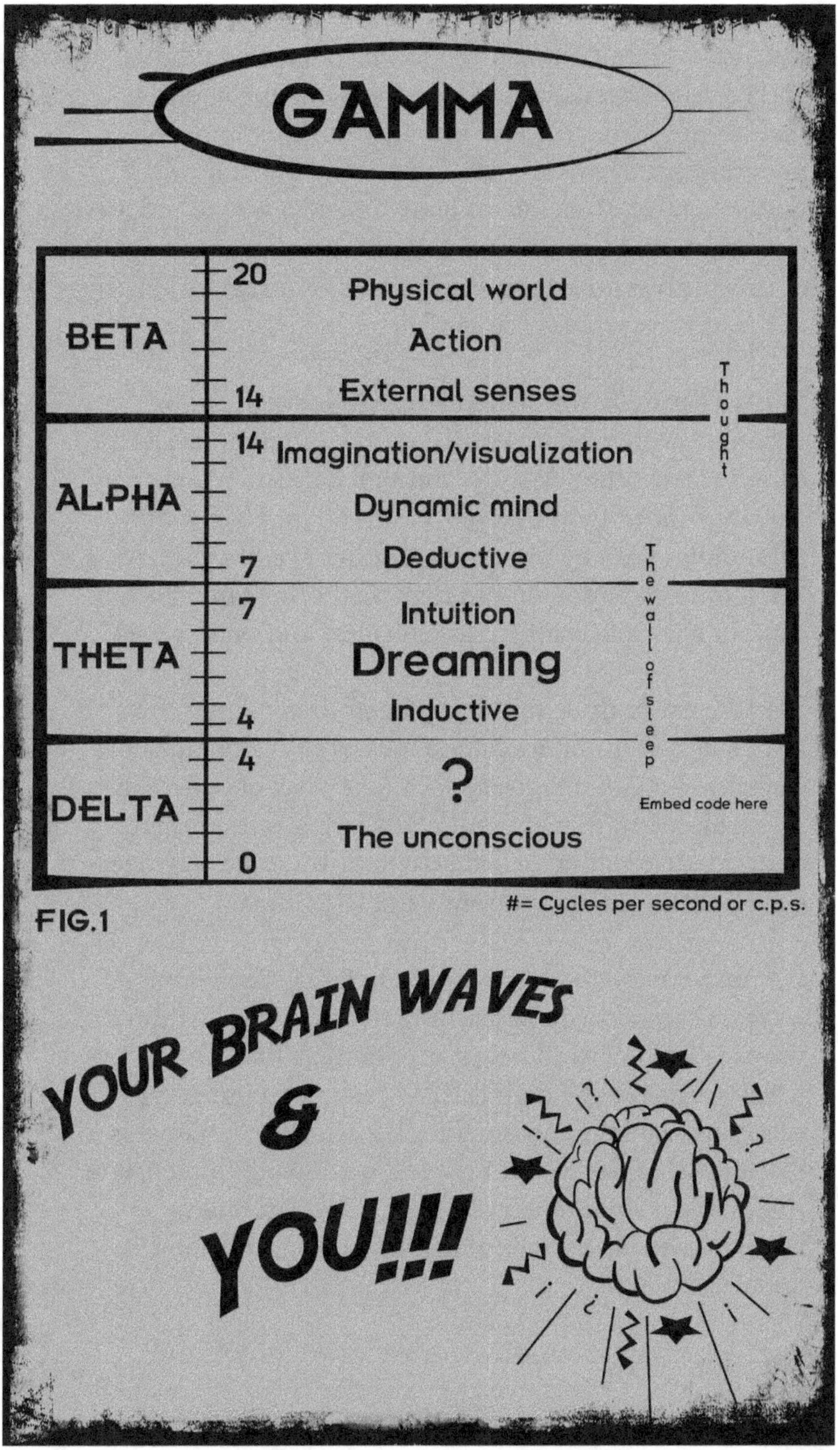

BETA	20	Physical world	
		Action	
	14	External senses	Thought
ALPHA	14	Imagination/visualization	
		Dynamic mind	
	7	Deductive	The wall of sleep
THETA	7	Intuition	
		Dreaming	
	4	Inductive	
DELTA	4	**?**	
			Embed code here
		The unconscious	
	0		

FIG.1

#= Cycles per second or c.p.s.

YOUR BRAIN WAVES & YOU!!!

The reason that I am adding this explanation to the end of this section is that I have been talking about manifesting your true will throughout this snippet of my grimoire. I have spoken about why your true will is important, how to come to know it, and a way to manifest it in line with your desire. I gained a better understanding of this process and made it a little less esoteric by looking at it from a psychological model.

What I mean by this is that I started looking at how our mind works, brain waves, and the different levels of consciousness that we cycle through consistently every day. It is understood that our brains are incredible and mysterious. I am by no means an expert on the human brain but I have done more than a bit of research and experiments concerning consciousness and brain waves.

My interest in these topics is related to my desire to rewire myself. Brain waves are measured fluctuations of electrical potential between different parts of our brains. These electrical rhythms pulse at varying rates of speed or cycles depending on some factors. There are 5 known wavelengths cycling up from delta to gamma.

Gamma waves are small amplitude quick frequency waves. Discovering and learning to understand gamma waves is leading to some great potential. Until the development of the digital EEG recorder gamma rays were not visible or measurable. The gamma wave seems to unite all of the parts of the brain allowing the separate pieces to act simultaneously. In this state of brain wave activity we have bright flashes of intuition and understanding.

An example of this may be if you have ever experienced what feels like a substantial slowing down of time. I have been in car accidents and other high-stress events where it appears that time has slowed down to an incredible rate. Details become vivid and the moment becomes extra lucid. It is a heightened state of awareness.

In the process of sigilization I believe it may be the gamma waves that inspire the concept and that the actual ritual induces gamma brain wave activity but those waves are not where the information is embedded. The information is buried deep in your unconscious mind in the delta wave rhythm. The delta brainwave is the lowest known frequency of brain wave activity.

Let's start where most of us spend a majority of our conscious cycle. The beta wave rhythm. Beta is the cycle of most basic waking mental activity. Time spent being attentive, actively listening, and problem-solving, occur in the beta rhythm. Even though beta happens when we are conscious we are also simultaneously experiencing a beta wave frequency while we sleep. Beta waves occur during REM sleep. Beta waves are present in the parts of the brain which regulate motor control including eye movement. Think of a time when you are relaxed and have your eyes closed. The stillness that you are feeling is in part due to entering into an alpha brain rhythm. I consider cycling into the alpha brain rhythm as taking the 1st step of entering into magical time. Coming into an alpha state happens naturally. Consciously intending to put yourself in an alpha state is an act of creating change in conformity with the true will.

Change in conformity with the will is my definition of magic. The conscious act of bringing desired results. Alpha brain frequency is the territory that lies right at the edge of our imagination. Our creative thoughts start to form here. Our daydreaming and sleep dreaming minds flow to the alpha rhythm. The possibility for magik begins in alpha frequency because our logical minds are toned down a bit leaving us open and susceptible to suggestion.

At the point that we enter into theta frequency, we may be cycling as low as 4 to 7 Hz. Theta is where we space out. Theta frequency cycle is just above unconsciousness. The best example of this is going on a long drive and suddenly arriving at your destination with no recollection of the trip. Traveling in a straight line down a long featureless highway induces theta wave frequency.

The idea of being on autopilot or going through the motions of repetitive tasks belongs in the realm of theta brain wave activity. Theta frequency is where psychic and paranormal experiences are perceived. Theta frequency is where we are very receptive to external, internal, and extrasensory perception. We become aware of subtle energies and influences in this state. Theta occurs right before delta, so theta is right at the edge of consciousness.

Know we pierce the wall of sleep. Delta frequency is the dark, dreamless depths of the unconscious. Brain wave activity is usually measured between 4 and 0 Hz in this state. As far as we know our bodies and minds are at complete rest in delta rhythm. Our unconscious mind is just that. Unconscious. In this part of our minds is where we embed the code for a sigil.

Think of a link on a website. The code for the link is on the index page of the site that is inside of your root folder. Even though the link is visible on the page you click. The actual code that creates the connection and carries you to its destination is embedded in the root folder on the index page. Below the virtual surface and deep in the code of the website the message is embedded. Creating, activating, and launching a sigil, is very similar to embedding code or writing HTML, CSS, PHP, or any other type of system. The steps that are taken to create the Sigil are what inserts the code into our unconscious mind where it is recalled from and launched into mundane reality to manifest the desire that it represents.

The idea is to try to become lucid in each cycle of brainwave frequency. Becoming aware and lucid while experiencing our different brain wave activity allows us to glean new information consciously from our altered states. Think of lucid dreaming. Some people are natural lucid dreamers but for most of us it takes work. Over time and practice you can become a lucid dreamer. The same concepts can be used in the more subtle practice of becoming conscious of our brain wave activity and consciously interacting, with our minds in these states.

Ritual magik, sigil magik, meditation, spirituality, and any other practice that pushes the boundaries of our experience are what makes us evolve as individuals and a species. I think it is important for each of us to explore our potential and understanding.

DEATH

A=△ I=ϕ Q=⊙ Y=→

B=⌐∧ J=⌐ R=⊢ Z=●♂

C=◯⊢ K=< S=—〜

D=↑ L=━ T=+

E=⌐ M=╫ U=—c

F=⌐ N=⅃ V=⤙

G=♋ O=● W=▽

H=⊤ P=⌐ X=⊼

MAGIC

SEX

The Grammar of the Bizarre

The Paranormal

2016 INTERMISSION 2017

It is Christmas day, 2016. I am sitting at my kitchen table with my wife. She is watching a show on Netflix about Australian border security. We have just pulled an amazing looking lasagna out of the oven. We are letting it cool down before we make some salads to go along with what smells like a fantastic entree. We also have some French bread that we have coated and slathered with a delicious garlic and Parmesan cheese butter infused with all kinds of savory herbs.

I mean after all what is lasagna without garlic bread and salad? On a much darker note just a few hours ago we left my grandmother in laws house. Only a few short days ago she passed away peacefully. She made great contributions to this world and was one of the most respected people I have known. I take a look at my wife. She is staring at her hands that are folded in front of her on the table. The Australian border show is droning on in the background from her tablet. I guess she feels me looking at her and she says, "I don't think I am starving."

I acknowledge this and start thinking about just how brutal 2016 has been for so many people. 2016 was a year when the impossible became possible. The Chicago Cubs won The World Series. It is certainly a year that has been full of tragedy, celebrity death, and strange events for us all. It seems like has been truly out to get us.

Just today we celebrated our first Christmas without my wife's grandmother. On top of that George Micheal died. Oddly enough I was just talking about how I always wondered what he meant by "You let the sunshine out of my hands!" Unless George Micheal comes to me in a fitful dream, filled with ultra short blue jean shorts and neon bandannas, I may never know. I will not go too far in the annals of death in 2016. Just look up the year, and you will see for yourself.

For those of you who manage to scrape by with little to no damage the death of some influential artists, actors, actresses, and musicians had to give you at least a couple gut punches. On top of that in America we had one of the strangest most bizarre presidential election sagas, maybe ever. We all know how that turned out. We saw the natives at Standing Rock protest the expansion of oil pipelines that encroached upon the safety of their precious and life-sustaining natural resources.

We saw them get the hose and the dogs. We saw them get sprayed with chemicals. We saw black lives matter stir the pot and become recognized. The KKK, Neo-Nazi, and, other white supremacy groups managed to get their feet and hands in the door before it could slam on them. People told so many lies that we probably heard the horrible truth being told and did not believe it.

People became obsessed with the idea that Mercury retrograde was running rampant over their lives. Using the term Mercury retrograde became a way to explain things going wrong. The suspension of logic and reason and the need to deflect the responsibility of tragedy on external factors seemed to become a general mindset. Everyone got butt hurt about something. I for one have become fed up with the term millennial and how they are blamed for ruining the world that created them.

2016 was one of the most paranormal years that I have lived. I am sitting here at a table that once belonged to my wife's grandma. I am wrapping up a project I started about ten months ago. Even though I grossly underestimated the amount of time it would take to complete this project it is coming to an end. Just like 2016. So as the year ends and we go into an unknown territory full of spinning possibility and mystery our journey here reflects that. As above so below.

The paranormal is the study of what is outside of the standard, measurable, and consensual understanding that defines quantifiable reality. What is defined as paranormal changes with time? My in-laws were kind enough to get us a nice present this year for Christmas. They got us an Alexa Echo Dot. You can ask Alexa questions and she will answer them. Alexa's function is vast and yet to be explored but 100 years ago this would be something close to magic. Today you can buy it on Amazon for a great price from the comfort of your home. What sorcery!

The more technology we have the stranger society becomes. Achievable reality expands past a point of understanding just how much we can achieve. I feel that even though I enjoy taking advantage of the technology I avoid an obsession or dependence on technology. Just like I avoid dependence on always using occult means to gain an end.

The paranormal seems just to be a school of science that we are trying to learn to quantify. There is little to no empirical data to build. Other than what we experience and can capture by whatever medium is used, there is nothing. I am a big tent paranormalist. I feel that the paranormal is greater than ghosts. There are a few schools of interest in the overall field. Many people claim that ufology is more real than ghosts and other subjects concerning spirits and the like.

This attitude seems to stem from the idea that ufology can be proven by conventional scientific means. Debris and other evidence left at hot spots and crash sites are in fact concrete proof. If you can find it, there are a lot of tangible physical objects and evidence that could be analyzed. There are scientific concepts that can explain space travel. I guess this makes ufology less paranormal to some. Theories are just as varied in the field of ufology as they are in the study and investigation of ghosts and spirits.

Some ancient alien theorist give all of the credit to god-like extraterrestrial bein , for anything significant in human history. Doesn't this relegate people to bleating morons who have always had to be guided step by step and have never achieved greatness on their own? Why couldn't Leonardo Da Vinci have just been a genius mastermind? I believe in the ancient alien theory but I can not believe that human beings have not accomplished any thing on their own.

Giving away to the idea, that we are no more than just a germ like a pestilence in the multiverse has got to be bad for the old self-esteem. I am not afraid to think that maybe some extraterrestrials are not so helpful. Even though they may be evolved and unified as a species or culture. They could very well be bent on the complete and total annihilation of star systems.

Look I am just a graphic designer, occultist, and general mis-manager of my world. I am not going to attempt to put myself in league with a physicist like Stephen Hawkins but I am a living thinking human being that has put a lot of thought and action into the study of the paranormal. I have interviewed authors, historians, cult leaders, black magicians, witches, retired army officials, whistle blowers, and other freaks, geeks, and weirdos. One of the main things I have gathered is that we are just barely scratching the surface. I still say we might be close but the real truth is far beyond what we currently perceive.

Another field of study that I put under my big tent is cryptology or the study of specific crytpids like Bigfoot. When I was consistently doing shows with Jeffery Pritchett at The Church of Mabus radio show, I think we spent a good 10 or 13 months doing mostly cryptid themed shows. We talked to a wide variety of experts, experiencers and people who had some pretty far out stories to tell. What I noticed was just how varied and divided this field was as well. All in all Bigfoot was the main course of our interviews.

We occasionally talked about an eclectic group of terrifying nightmarish creatures who stalk the land by night and wreaked general havoc on communities and individuals. The grass man, dog man, lizard man, moth man, all types of creature men. We spoke of giants, hobbits, dragons, and other great and terrible monstrosities. But it always boiled down to Bigfoot. 1 of my favorites was a tale told by a person I will not name mostly because I do not remember who it was.

This story unfolded in a manner that put our guest in line with a search and recovery mission of a Sasquatch who had crash-landed on Earth on the way to Mars. Apparently Sasquatch is a terrible space pilot. Part of the mission included scuba diving to the location of the Sasquatch and his ship. At the point of discovery our storyteller and the team he was working with were to secure the craft to a crane cable so that the craft could be hoisted from the water, placed on a flatbed truck, and transported to parts unknown.

In the meantime our reluctant frogman had a particular job. Our guest was to retrieve the body of the Sasquatch. This entailed opening the hatch of the ship as it was right on the top of the craft and made of a transparent glass substance. Our particular Bigfoot was strapped into a cockpit dead as dead can be of what can be guessed as the impact of the crash.

After opening the craft hatch and securing the carcass. Our guest told us that he inserted a type of flotation device into the ass of the Sasquatch and pulled the cord to inflate the device so the Sasquatch could dreamily float to the surface where it could be retrieved by a small boat deployed directly over the ship...I am a guy who has seen a lot. Probably too much to mention and some things I can not believe myself. So I am asking myself is this shit for real?

The person telling the story seemed to believe that this had happened. Other than this being one of the most bizarre tales I have ever been told and expected to believe. It is an account of just how varied this view and experience is from those in this community who believe Bigfoot is simply a lost primate or something along those lines. To some Bigfoot is a highly evolved being who can shapeshift, teleport, and possesses magical powers. Some cultures view the hairy man as a shaman who has great wisdom. Whatever the case a lot of people debate it.

Even though an interest and acceptance of the paranormal continues to grow, peoples lives and reputation can be ruined over being involved or admitting to doing anything more than having a personal interest in the study of the paranormal. I think that some of these researchers, anthropologist, and scientists involved in a "serious" study of Bigfoot have to lean heavily on already established notions and laws to determine and quantify Sasquatch as a species. That way we can make them real.

It seems just like ghosts, aliens, and other nouns associated with the paranormal. Bigfoot lurks just outside of what is measurable. So it can not be quantified, regardless of what some would call irrefutable proof of the existence of this far out hairy hominid. I know they are real, maybe someday I will tell you why, but for now, let's keep moving ever forward to the end of our time together on this journey.

The next chapter you are about to read has a couple of my memorable experiences. We are also going to talk about shadow people, the hat man, reptilian, mantids, and gray aliens, and a few more strange and terrifying things. The next chapter is full of a variety of paranormal tidbits. We will discuss sleep paralysis and what could be paranormal overtones that are linked to the phenomena. Sleep paralysis can be scary enough to kill.

There is much to discuss and more pages to turn. By the end of this you may have some answers. You may also find some things that sound familiar. I know I am not the only person who has seen a shadow person. The hat man lurks in the corner of our minds, waiting for a chance to get in.

It is time for me to chop those salads and make this bread delicious. It seems that my wife is feeling hungry again. I am not surprised considering that she has hardly eaten in days. Grief will get you right in the gut as I am sure you know. At the time of our proximity to death the unseen world is beaming directly onto us. The effect is only a reflection of the dark mysterious beyond we can occasionally glimpse. Our grief is always a reflection of how much we love and the pain of the human condition. I think back to countless abysmal hours I have spent in hospitals and funeral homes. Any place an individual is close to the end of their time. In these locations shadows hang lower and seem to cling to places where there should normally be light. Long silences fill up corridors, hallways, and cramped rooms that are filled with spirits and crackling energy. I see that thing that I always see flitting around corners and hovering over the prone bodies of those who are about to pass.

Even at the times where I have been at the weird place at the odd time and have witnessed car crashes or other atrocious disasters. At times when I have pulled people out of crashed cars or have been there by synchronicities. It is still there. Just off to one side or the other until I turn and stand still. At that time it expands, and shows what seems to be a proximity to its actual shape. It is not a scary thing even though it scared me as a child. It is just there. Consistent. I agree with that angry German philosopher. You know who I mean. When you stare into the abyss, it will look back.

Beezle Alhazred
12/25/2016

But I do believe in the paranormal, that there are things our brains just can't understand. - Art Bell

I remember sitting in my townhouse. I was talking to my wife who is my best friend. The year was around 1998. We were talking about how the topic and the field of the paranormal seemed to be becoming more and more popular We had been watching shows like Sightings and listening to Art Bell and Coast to Coast. Sure enough, it happened. A few years later Ghost Hunters the ScyFy original series aired.

Not long after that,the paranormal blew up. I am a fan of spiritualism, spirit communication, and the spiritualist movement. It seems like the early 2000s to now have been a new type of era revival for the paranormal. Of course, the interest is waning and there are fewer and fewer paranormal shows being produced in Holywood...

Nowadays the big deal is Alaska, moonshine, and border security. I can't wait for the ghost hunting, Alaskan moonshiner, paranormal team, that works for border security as a day job. You know it could happen. While we might be losing paranormal TV we seem to be gaining a lot of radio shows and pod-casts.

In my opinion paranormal radio and pod-casts are better sources of information depending on the source. Understand I am not taking the amount of work and dedication it takes to make a fruitful reliable show for granted. Those who do it independently seem to benefit from the added revenue if the show is marketed well.

In any case that is just my opinion. Let's move forward. Time to get to the meat of it. I am going to talk about the thing that got me. The terror the memory that is burned into my peripheral vision. Just off to the side it lurks and gibbers. I am going to tell you about the paranormal experience which set me on this path to the bizarre. The experience that I am going to recall is my first encounter with the reality of shadow people.

I spent most of my childhood in a duplex style home. The house was built around the early 1940's. The property belonged to a family who had a house that was on the top of a hill. The property was secluded and cut off from the main road by small to medium size swaths of lush forestry. Our drive started at the bottom of the hill on Starky road in Zionsville, Indiana. Our house sat at the midpoint of the hill and we were tucked back pretty far off of the road.

We were the weird family in town. Kids never came up our driveway on Halloween. Our house was the haunted house that everyone shunned. If you grew up in a small town you know which 1 I am talking about. My mother was Native American, and my father was born in India and raised in Pakistan during the depression era.

There were more than a few reasons people were superstitious of us. The property we lived on backed up to a sewage treatment plant. There is a long sordid history involved with the property and my family but that is for another time.

There were numerous times as a child that I am sure I experienced a wide variety of paranormal phenomena. I just don't think that it dawned on me what it was that was happening until that sleepless unnerving night. I come from a large family as it turns out I did not have a fixed place to sleep or designated room at this point in my life.

On this specific sleepless night,I found myself in a bedroom that was in the middle of the house. My parents slept in there most of the time but they were posted up in the front room for some reason. I was laying there in a single bed next to a closet with no door. The space inside always seemed darker than it should be even in the daylight.

Across from me was a large plate glass window. In front of that off to the side a bit was a dresser with a small Zenith television sitting on its edge. The moon was full. I was peering in wonder from my bed out of the window into the great twilight. The vibrant light of the moon started to diminish as a large cloud lumbered over the front yard. While the view of my garden washed out under the inky black darkness that was traveling under that dense cloud. A vague shape started to form in front of the dresser.

The nightmare before me grew into a dark translucence and took on a vaguely humanoid shape. I was nailed to that single bed in that corner next to that closet. The insidious chill that rolled off of the adumbration that manifested there bit into the absolute fiber of my being. I was in such a state of horror that I could not even close my eyes. In an attempt to look past the shadow being I only saw a Stygian impenetrable gloom blooming behind it. It seemed like nothing was outside of the window anymore.

My mind broke a little more. I could not scream. I could hear Barney Miller blaring out of the floor model RCA television in the next room. My parents were getting blazed and cracking up about something. There we were. All night long. I laid there unable to move, speak, or hardly breathe. The creature hung there until eventually, a little bit of light started creeping in behind it. As the room filled with light the translucence gave way to a vague transparency. The more the creature faded the more its hold over me diminished.

I blacked out. When I came to, my dog was licking me and my mom was working to wake me up. She was concerned because I have always been a notoriously light sleeper. I felt terrible like I had the flu. As it turns out, I was running a fever and was dehydrated. I did not have any answers. I never told anybody what happened until much later. I had several other encounters, with what I believe was the same creature before I left that house forever.

A depiction of the shadow person who haunted me as a child. The sleep paralysis that I experienced during this paranormal ordeal is not uncommon to shadow people encounters. In some cases an old hag accompanies the shadow person. The old hag sits on your chest and steals your breath and vitality. Although there are similarities in shadow people encounters each occurrence is a singular, personal and terrifying event. Some people even develop PTSD due to the frequency and intensity of their encounters.

(Shadow People) What are they? We can only guess. Typically shadow people encounters appear to be negative or neutral. Hell even if they are friendly we would never know because of how terrifying they are. There is no doubt in my mind they are real. The unexplainable always yields up two choices for me. Either I am crazy and utterly delusional or this stuff is happening. I can accept both ideas.

What shadow people are is open for debate. I describe a shadow person as a negative energy entity. I am along the lines of thinking they tend to be malefic or darkly neutral. In my model they are not necessarily human spirits or energy but something else altogether that is otherworldly and multi-dimensional. Knowing what I know and thinking shadow creatures are autonomous beings with their own agendas. I believe it is possible other negative energy entities occasionally take the shape of a shadow for effect or to obscure their real identities.

Investigators and individuals have found other negative energy entities, like demons, Djinn, and other nasties will take on the form of other supernatural entities which are not so obviously evil. Doing this makes it easier for people to become fascinated and eventually obsessed. So the rabbit could be a monkey in disguise. To imitate something it has to be recognizable for it to be deceiving. So it has to have its own identity to be imitated.

People equate them to being an individual who was evil in life. I don't mean a crabby old racist neighbor evil. I mean kid killing, puppy punching evil. Something nasty. People who in life were filled with an impenetrable darkness and needed to intimidate and terrify others to feel powerful. Not just the garden variety bully but an actual psychopath. One who relishes in the act of terror. I have met a few people who like to entertain the idea they are viewed as more evil than they are. It seems to give them a little thrill.

In some cases shadow people could be the intended result of occult and psychic means. The shadow person could be the astral form of an individual or an astral entity designed to vex or protect an individual. Seeing through the eyes of creatures or objects is truly an ancient concept. Even seeing through your mind's eye as a remote viewer could produce an entity phenomena.

Thought forms, egregores, and even spirit familiars may be sent forth by those both with and without the proper understanding. In most cases these entities manifest as shadow beings or dark specters, vaguely human, translucent ghosties that appear to be shadow people. In fact in the previous section of the book we discuss sigilization. In my particular model of magic creating sigils is the base work needed to build advanced thought forms.

.

A widely popular theory is shadow people come straight from the bowels of hell. They are entities that sit at the Devils red right hand. Shadow entities are sent to torment and harass the blasphemous. In the Judea Christian mythology, heaven represents the light world and hell is the opposite in every aspect. Shadow people are considered to be 100% demonic by people of particular faiths. Every culture has an embodiment of these beings because all known cultures live in a world of light, dark, and shadow.

Some paranormal investigators consider "shadow" to be a type of spiritual condition. A shadow creature is a lost human spirit. In this model shadow people are just scarred confused souls,wandering in either an intelligent or residual shadow state. Shadow people defined as ghosts are often skittish and avoid people as much as possible. Just like the mega-evil human we described earlier. A sad confused, faithless, or lost person could manifest as a shadow entity in death. These entities are in a plane of purgatory, neutrality, and the undecided.

Shadow people also tend to be just at the corner of your eye. Experiencers say over time a shadow would appear in their peripheral vision. Until eventually the shadow appears directly in front of them. Psychosis and side effects cannot be ruled out either. The side effects associated with the pharmaceutical and even holistic drugs and treatments cannot be ignored. It seems that most people are hopped up on something.

(Sleep Paralysis) is often used to explain some of these experiences. People are starting to think that sleep paralysis is caused by shadow people. Sleep paralysis is a product of a natural physiological process. Sleep paralysis is not an uncommon experience for people. In fact, it happens to all of us when we enter REM sleep. If this did not occur we would probably not sleep well and seriously hurt ourselves.

For a long tim, scientists had no idea what chemicals our brains create,that causes this paralysis. A few years ago a team of scientists from The University of Toronto discovered the neurotransmitters known as glycine, working together with a chemical known as GABA. The combination of the 2 is what seems to cause muscle paralysis during REM sleep. That was quite an exciting discovery. What happens is that people will cycle up through the levels of sleep to fast and become conscious while in a natural state of sleep paralysis. The hypnogogic state is where we are potentially the most lucid while sleeping and dreaming. Transitioning to the hypnopompic state to rapidly causes quite a bit of disorientation.

So science likes to dictate the old hag and shadow people experience are the cause of sleep disorders. I am of the mind that it is possible that being in that state while we are conscious allows us a glimpse into the unseen world. Maybe being in that state permits us to see the terrifying entities just at the edge of our conscious mind. Understandably, even if all of this is just a trick of the mind, paranoia, sleep deprivation, and constant terror, will drive someone mad.

Parasomnia are sleep-related hallucinations. People who are narcoleptic, experience sleep attacks, sleep paralysis, and hypnogogic hallucinations. Whatever the case we keep digging up questions. Doctors relegate this phenomenon to sleep disorders and physiological processes because that is what they know and how they understand these hallucinations. People have died or feel like they are going to die while they are in a state of wakeful sleep paralysis. Some individuals, who have sleep paralysis describe symptoms of having a stroke or a heart attack.

Sufferers have been unable to breathe in these states and the effort it takes to bring yourself out of the paralysis, is tremendous. If you are even able to. Linking an archetypal fear-based entity to a particular disorder is very peculiar but not unexpected. Across the world that we know cultures, societies, and faiths have the same experiences. It seems shadow people are a very personal reflection. Even what we project and the exact nature of our psychological and physiological characteristics are a true mystery to us.

I am sure the future yields some startling truths and revelations concerning the nature of our unconscious minds. I for one would like to than, all of the rats who have been and will be completely rewired to make these discoveries. I know and many other people know there is more to it at least sometimes.

(Hat Man) is a particular typically very aggressive shadow person. People have attempted suicide to escape Hat Man's oppression. Most individuals who describe a Hat Man encounter describe a meeting with a barren entity cold and foul to the rotten malevolent core. A real pit of menace and degradation. Hat man seems to be a boss to the typical shadow person. Some people even describe Hat Man murdering lesser shadow entities, in front of them to illicit that thick black inky fear that boils up from their DNA.

It seems that fear and terror are the aid and succor to the shadow people. Hat Man is known to torment, abuse, and drive its victims beyond a point of sanity. Hat Man is as timeless as it is terrifying. We see examples of this creature in more than a few cultures. The legendary dream murderer, Freddy Krueger: a Hat Man if I have ever seen one. Pop culture provides immortality for legend and superstition. Hat Man also appears in conjunction with alien abduction experiences as well.

I have been in 2 locations where I encountered a very high level of shadow people activity. At Waverly Hills Sanatorium there was so much activity it was undeniable of what you were seeing. Blatant shadow people business. Hat Man encounters seem to increase in locations where there is a significant frequency of shadow activity.

What you see here is one 1 of the 999 frames, I captured in the video ITC experiment, I conducted in the basement of Bobby Mackey's Country Music World. There appears to be a strange form emerging from the image.

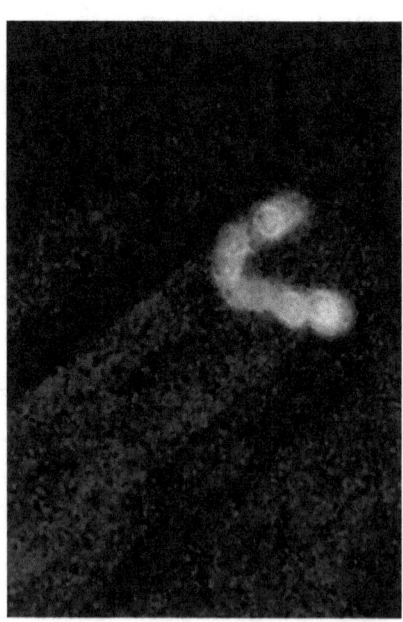

!!!UNRELATED BONUS!!!
IMAGE

We captured the bonus image at the same investigation. We used a simple disposable camera. We shot the picture in a sequence of random photos. What you are seeing is a shot of the dance floor and a strange anomaly. Other investigators have claimed to have seen a strange figure in that area, that resembles a centipede. Psychic investigators have reported seeing an astral insectoid entity, skittering around, and climbing the walls and ceilings in the same area. Could this be an image of such a creature?

After we set up the experiment at Bobby Mackey's, we waited for a few minutes to let everything sink in before we took off on the ITC capture. I find when I am conducting spirit communication experiments and I just let everything sit there for few minutes. I start to notice a clearer connection between the environment, the equipment, and what it is I intend to do.

Announcing your intentions while setting up an experiment is also helpful. Perhaps speaking your plans and making them known gives the whole process a little boost and potentially draws contact with willing energy entities, who want to talk. When creating a controlled environment do your best to mark as many details, that you feel are viable about the event you are managing.

A little bit of time goes by. We tick off the boxes and cross off the lists. We collect our preliminary investigation data and decide to get started. The time is approximately 4:37 pm. Okay so back in Indiana my wife was in our kitchen tidying up before she prepared a hot meal for herself. Right after we started the experiment she said that she was standing at the sink and felt something behind her.

When she turned around she saw a vague shadowy form which resembled the form that seems to be emerging from the background of the image on the previous page. She described a tall figure who appeared to be wearing a hat. My wife is one of the most powerful people I have ever met. She only advised Hat Man to return from whence he came before she had to get angry about it. Get the fuck out of here before you piss me off. That is what she said. Apparently Hat Man GTFO.

My wife sent me a text message directly after her experience. I turned my phone off before we set up the experiment and I did not receive the message until we left town. At the time that the entity appeared in my dining room I was at Bobby Mackey's requesting for the hat wearing entity to make itself known through one of the means of communication we had provided. Weird? You are god damn right that is weird.

Jenny had accompanied me on my preliminary investigation of Bobby Mackey's. I will usually conduct an initial inquiry of a location before I decide rather or not I should set up a larger team experiment. This way I can craft a particular study depending on the type of talent I want to get involved. I trust my wife more than anyone. She is proven to be highly intuitive and has shown clairvoyant abilities.

The first time we were there she described seeing and sensing a wide variety of energy entities including Hat Man. Could Hat Man have traveled to our house in Indiana from the basement of Bobby Mackey's via some gateway? Was the experience that my wife had related to the experiment at Bobby Mackey's? I think yes to both. There are too many connecting factors. Hat Man and shadow appear in locations that are considered, to have a high frequency of paranormal activity. Either as a cause or effect one always seems to follow the other.

Opinions vary but not widely. Those that hold shadow people to a degree of being protectors, watchers or helpful entities may be right as well. I guess it just depends on our own experiences. Out of all known possible phenomena that could occur. I have had the most exposure to shadow entities. Other than the series of events I described at the Bobby Mackey's ITC experiment. I have not had any other known experiences with Hat Man. . .

If all of the events that I described earlier are related and Hat Man was somehow able to travel from the basement of Bobby Mackey's Country Music World to my dining room. Those events add credence to the idea that Hat Man is a viral entity. By viral entity I mean an entity that travels from person to person place to place utilizing association or mentioning. Speak of the devil and the devil appears.

Is there more than 1 Hat Man? I think so. Unless Hat Man is omnipresent then that would have to be the case. Do we know if Hat Man is ubiquitous? Of course not. Could 1 Hat Man be plaguing all of its victims individually by somehow transporting all over the world? That does not seem likely. I can not say that it is impossible considering the paranormal nature of the topic.

Hat Man and shadow people are cross-genre entities. You will find references to the entities in the mystical, ghostly, apparition, entity, and ufology categories of the paranormal. My big tent is full but I can always make room for more. I have limited experience when it comes to ufology. Other than seeing a few unidentified flying objects or beyond my lifetime work on communication, with the entities, related to the Lovecraft mythos and Simon's Necronomicon. I do not believe I have had any or very many direct experiences. Why don't we take a quick shadow entity respite while I recount a time when Jenny and I saw a strange thing in the sky! Our intermission is entitled ---

SOMETHING STRANGE IN THE SKY!!!

Another necessary distraction-
There is nothing more important in
The study of the paranormal
Than real life experience

All of the experiences reported in
This volume, are accurate to the
Exact point of detail that could be
Recalled in the telling

It is important to study and document
All data concerned with all experiments,
Experiences, and investigations
That you conduct

It seems that the most compelling
Experiences always occur at a time
That you are completely unprepared
To document them

There's nothing
More satisfying than a group
Experience

I am pretty sure it was late September of 1998. Jenny and I were rolling around in her 1977 Ford Thunderbird. The exterior silver paint glinted dully in the light of the vibrant Fall sun. We were sitting comfortably in our red leather bench seat. The armrest was down and Jenny was resting her right arm on it, while she was casually steering with her left hand at the 12 O'clock position. I was looking into the passenger side mirror contemplating the message printed on the glass.

Objects in the mirror may appear closer than they are. I have always thought that was strange for some reason. We were idly chatting about our purchases we had made at Half Price Books and Barnes and Nobles. Our destination was Westfield, Indiana. I am pretty sure we were headed there to visit with Jenny's mom and possibly have dinner. We were out at a wrong time to be on the road in this part of town. Traffic was heavy. We had a bit of gridlock by I-465 and Keystone Avenue.

Trapped on all sides by the crawling chaos we idled. Indiana weather is notoriously unpredictable. So predictably the weather took a turn for the ominous. Mountainous thunderheads manifested pregnant with rain and lighting. The air was getting charged, and the wind gusted violently into the T'bird's heavy metal carcass and massive windows. Traffic anxiously lurched forward for about 15 feet or so then we idled again.

We had some quick nervous chatter between us clumsily rolled our windows most of the way up and fired up a smoke. We love storms but this storm had a distinct aura. People talk about UFOs using clouds as cover to hide in plain sight. There is more to this than just talk. People also speculate that sudden storms and UFO activity are linked under specific conditions. One way or the other, we did not see what you might think of when I say UFO.

Traffic was moving at an agonizing hurry up and wait tempo. Since the clouds had rolled in there had been short bursts of intense rain. At one point, when we were entirely stopped. A sudden palpable calm occurred outside of the comfortable leather seat of the Thunderbird. The wind seemed to stop so suddenly. The leaves and trash that were blowing around appeared to be suspended in the air before they fluttered to the ground.

Jenny asked me if I saw something strange in the sky. She was looking to the North East towards the I-465 overpass on Keystone Avenue. I had no idea what she was seeing. I leaned over and took a look out of her window. At first I did not see anything, but then I saw it. Off in the distance out of the bottom of a massive thundercloud. Something came twisting out

At first it resembled a giant sewer tubing like you might see in drainage ditches on the side of the road. We were stopped for at least 3 or 4 minutes and traffic moved another 15 or 20 feet. Moving forward allowed us a different perspective.

We were gob stopped. What were we seeing? It started moving in a very purposeful fashion farther away to the North. Keep in mind in Indiana in the area it would have been directly over is mostly farmland and The City of Carmel. People in the city would have been indoors or just leaving work at this time. What we were seeing was gigantic because it looked huge from pretty far away.

The more I looked at it the more it appeared to be alive! I dare say it seemed like some great Wyrm whose coils were dipping in and out of the clouds. Maybe not quite reptilian but defiantly not like any single thing that I have ever seen before. In my mind it was utterly alien. We cackled madly as our minds broke a little with the possibility that seemed to be right before us.

Traffic moved again. We started to pick up the pace a bit. Our minds were racing trying to make sense of this. Was it a piece of a banner from an airplane advertisement that became loose? Could it have been a huge wacky waving inflatable tube man launched off of its air compressor? Or was it some piece of the gigantic sky...Trash? No, it was not any of those. By all intents and purposes, it appeared to be some eldritch thing. Something that did not belong in this particular sky. Traffic seemed to be picking up. Jenny had to get her eyes back on the road. I looked around for a second as we picked up speed. I saw a few people looking in the direction of the thing in the sky.

I looked back and it had moved much farther away. I saw it roll and saw what appeared to be a large tattered wing unfold from its side as it disappeared into another cloud. We were heated basically busting out of our bodies with excitement and wonder. In yet another strange twist of weather the clouds started to disperse and the sunset began to cut the gloom with its golden rays.

Of course we tried to tell people what we say but most people just dismissed us and glossed over our mania. We have no idea what the hell that was. What we can agree on is that we saw the same thing something that appeared to be a monster. A creature.

What did we see? Did it come out of some craft hidden in the clouds? Did some dimensional gateway open and release some nightmarish entity into this world? Or were we and a few others having a collective acid flashback?

If the other people did see something, did they see the same thing we did? We never saw anything about it in the news. It is of course 100% possible it was something utterly mundane, and our minds just played us. We are relatively sure that this is not the case. We feel fortunate to have had this shared experience; it certainly fills us with a sense of terrific wonder and amazement.

END TRANSMISSION

When Hat Man appears in conjunction with ET abduction scenarios it is usually with the Mantid and Grey varieties of extraterrestrials. Let's look into those species briefly before we move on. Maybe that way we can gain some perspective.

(Greys) There is not enough room for this book to come close to fully discussing the Greys. Sometimes known as Zeta Reticulans. Give or take 39 light years from Earth is the constellation Zeta Reticulum. At the constellations Southern point spans a binary system called Zeta Reticuli. Many believe that Short Greys hail from this particular spot of our ever-expanding multiverse. Greys are related to some of the most infamous and well known episodes concerning Ufology.

We see Greys in connection with the ever famous Roswell incident. Greys are the most recognized species of extraterrestrial that comes to mind. The traditional small frame, large head, huge hands, big oval black eyes, and of course the grayish tint of what appears to be their skin. The movie Fire In The Sky the story of Travis Walton's abduction and eventual recovery centered on Greys as the extraterrestrials involved in the kidnapping of Travis Walton

The Greys are also known for being very active in the abduction of humans. On one of my favorite TV shows. The X Files. The Greys played a role in the overall main storyline of the show's lore. The human-alien hybrid theory is an agenda of Grey aliens.

Many people, apparently including Greys feel that the union is the next natural leap of evolution. Considering that we do not know or understand our DNA completely there is no way of knowing the implications of this union. I can't help but wonder what it is that these beings want to accomplish. Why would they be interested in creating such a hybrid? Is it their shortcomings or ours? I guess that it is a little bit of both.

Researchers, experiencers, and hardcore Ufologist all feel that extraterrestrials are far superior to human beings. When maybe part and parcel we are quite similar. Perhaps our DNA did not have its origins on this particular planet. I can only guess. But is it possible Greys would benefit just as much as we would with this jump in evolution? In any case the idea is quite bizarre indeed.

An example of this union are Tall Greys. Tall Greys are a combination of the DNA, of humans and Short Greys. Short Greys seem to be the foot soldiers of a larger Reptilian domination plan. Tall Greys are the beings that appear to be in charge of the more significant diplomatic relationships with various governments and institutions.

Where Short Greys are conducting most of the hands on dirty deeds. Tall Greys are considered a step up in the hierarchy of this alien species. A vast conspiracy that entails the idea that Greys and their Reptilian overlords have us all under a form of powerful mind control is often discussed and far-reaching.

The whole idea feels and sounds like 1 of my favorite movies. They Live. There is more than enough people who claim to believe too or simply have had too many real life experiences with these beings not to consider these notions to be a stark reality. As I mentioned earlier, I have talked to more than a few people who are convinced, that they are either abductee, inductees, and even hybrids. These beings subject people to some bizarre treatment and experimentation.

Some of my research pointed towards Greys conducting both bovine and human mutilation and exsanguination. There is a big question mark about why they do this. One idea is that they use the materials they extract for sustenance. How they ingest this ghoulish elixir is also up to speculation. 1 idea is that they rub the fluids on their skin and absorb it that way. An article that I found from 2009 by Brenden Borrell in Scientific America magazine states that a bizarre marine creature absorbs all of its nutrients through its skin.

The creatures are known as Ediacarans. Ediacarans are considered to be Earth's first complex organism. Today they could be compared to animals in the class Anthozoa of phylum Cnidaria and the phylum Porifera. Otherwise corals and sponges. Corals and Sponges only absorb some of their nutrients this way. The Ediacarans have no orifices and are of Pre-Cambrian or beyond in origin. It is challenging to compare these creatures to any known animal due to their unique and almost alien properties.

I have to consider that maybe the Ediacaran are proof of the remnants of the DNA of the extraterrestrials whose DNA we share. The Ediacaran are the first complex organism to form on Earth. The alien DNA could have been that boost or spark needed to create life as we know it and have yet to understand it. One way or the other the fact of the matter could be considered that Greys are experimenting, abducting, raping, and impregnating human beings.

I do not consider this to be proper behavior for what people think of highly evolved beings. People tell me. "Oh, you just don't understand." To them, I say, "Good day to you sir!" Considering many people would willingly participate with such alien escapades. Why all of the subterfuge?

(Mantids) are truly an enigma. Along with Hat Man, Short Grays, Tall Grays, and Reptilians, experiencers have reported mantis-like creatures observing their experience. These insectoid creatures are said to emit very positive, supportive, and comforting emotions. Mantids are sometimes directing the course of the event. These insectoid voyeurs are most commonly present during both the consensual and non-consensual sexual encounters.

The presence of the creatures at these particular events and their ability to project emotions onto people leads me to believe that they are intergalactic perverts that feed off of the energy of these activities or they are in charge of the whole operation. Mantids are considered to be the top of the chain of command.

There is a belief that Greys have mastered time travel. If you happened to be a captive or guest of a Grey, Reptilian, or Mantid alien, you could be anywhere in time or anywhere at all. One idea is that Mantids evolved here on Earth eons before our species. The Mantids travel from their past to our present time, or any point in time, that they need to be.

Many reports claim that Mantids are gentle and kind towards their captives and people who are experiencing these events. Mantids are universal project managers, who maintain standards, and regulations of these types of procedures and intergalactic group operations. Even though from this perspective Mantids appear to be great benefactors to our world. Not everyone has the same perception of these creatures.

Other accounts tell a tale of Mantids having a hybridization agenda. A plan that goes hand in hand with The Reptilian's nefarious plots. Some people living with sleep paralysis claim to see these creatures towering over them while they are in between sleep and wakefulness unable to move. In these cases the people who have claimed to have experienced this are full of a sense of absolute fear and terror. At this time in both sleep paralysis and abduction scenarios Mantids reveal their intentions as wanting to dominate and enslave our world.

So what does that leave us? What does Hat Man have to do with this? The Mantid hybridization agenda is said to produce a creature that is very tall, pitch black, and has glowing red eyes. This creature also seems to have the ability to capture people and hold them in a state of sleep paralysis. These hybrids are supposed to have very long arms and legs that have extra joints. The description of these creatures is very similar to Hat Man.

Perhaps Hat Man is an insectoid alien. Could it be that Mantids disguise themselves as shadow entities? Or are they just projecting from another dimension or a point in time and they are just not quite all the way here? Some Ufologist and paranormal investigators believe that all paranormal activity is the product of alien design. The real relationship Hat Man has with these creatures is unclear. I am sure whatever the reasons are they are bizarre indeed.

As time ticks on people are starting to accept that human beings are not the only advanced species in the multiverse. Even if all of this is just bullshit life very well could exist in forms that we simply do not understand. As I have said my experience in this field is limited but I have always believed that extraterrestrials are a reality. Rather or not they are our benevolent benefactors, our secret overlords, or a combination of both. Something is out there. Beings who exist just a bit off to the side. There is a theory that because when we realized as a species that the universe did not revolve around our planet. We have not entirely healed from the trauma of the realization. I think people try to hold on tightly to the idea that we are the most valid form of life in the universe. Maybe believing anything else is terrifying.

The word paranormal is a word that has an ever expanding possibility. Please understand that I know that people have suffered greatly at the clawed and probing hands of some grim realities. In my own life I have collected a wealth of personal, shared, and authentic paranormal experiences. Even at times when I believe that I have intentionally set forth supernormal events by occult means. That seem to have had an impact on an environment, object, person, or a scenario. I know there is a link, a strong bond that couples magic and the paranormal.

Aliens, ghosts, and shadow people are just as much of what makes human beings the most bizarre creatures of all. Some people truly believe that Greys are real. So what do Greys consider to be paranormal? How do they process death? Do they even consider the concept of anything being paranormal? If the paranormal is something outside of our understanding that defies explanation? Then what if there is very little that is outside of your actual knowledge?

Now think of beings like demons, djinn, angels, and even Gods and Goddesses. Beings that are eternal how vast is their understanding when time is not a factor. Out of all of the things that we believe to exist. All of the possibility that we can dream up and so many things that we have proven and will eventually understand. It is human beings who exist. People are real and proven beyond the shadow of a doubt. Our mark is large and sometimes not that beautiful. People are filled with all of the wonders in all of the worlds but we just may never really know.

THE END

Here is the end of our journey together. Our final stopping point. I hope that you have enjoyed the ride. I would like to think that you are a little sad that our time together is reaching its conclusion. That is because I may be a little sadistic. We have covered a lot of ground here. Snippets of broad topics that all seem to be related somehow. Murder, mystery, and mayhem are what we have in store for you. Thank goodness there are no shortages or deficits concerning these topics.

So what is the vehicle going to be that ushers us out of this contraption? Magic. Back in the occult section of this book I promised we would go over some means and techniques to help protect yourself from occult, supernatural, paranormal side effects, and dangers. So that is what we are going to do. No matter how many times it has to be said magic works. It is not the understanding and the study of magic that is always dangerous. It is the practice and application of magic that may protect you but also put you directly in line with forces that are outside of your experience.

Entering into a personal covenant of being a magician adds responsibility to our lives. Sometimes you can not undo the things that have happened. Personal responsibility is what is neede, in becoming judicious enough to know when to use magic and how to use magic. More often than not we see people approaching the topics of the occult and spirit communication with a sense of thrill seeking and entertainment.

We have all heard many tales of possession, hauntings, and other paranormal phenomena starting with "Well, we were playing with a Ouija board, or we tried to cast a spell from this book we found." So you put your incense and candles out, tidy up and move on to the next thing. Meanwhile what is not understood is that the act of performing the ritual has had an impact on an unseen or astral world.

If one of the greatest laws of magic is to know thy self then the hermetic axiom as above so below is just as significant. The statement describes a reflection or relationship between the micro and macrocosms within and without of all of us. Magik is brought forth from the unseen world in the form of the will and the intention behind the magic. We work to bring it through the aether. Magic is meaningless without intention. The more we perform the act in this world the closer we come to drawing the magik into reality.

What most people experience is a general lack of preparation and a great lack of understanding. More often than not we turn to fortune telling, casting spells, psychology, and even religion when we are at the end of our wits. After our problems are solved people tend to abandon the practices that led them to salvation. To be a practitioner you must continue, expand, and recognize the effects that magik has in our lives. Do these things that I am going to show you with a sense of purpose, practice, and a growing understanding. If you rely on these techniques to serve and protect you. They are going to have to become more than just words on a page in a weird book.

PREPARATION

Being prepared is important. Most of the time
preparation takes awareness of the need to be prepared.
I guess for me recognizing the potential danger around
me or knowing that if I am going to be involved with
some nouns that could yield unknown results. I might put
some planning into it. When I investigate, I have typically
visited the site before the investigation. If I am going to
a place I have not been able to feel out. I put myself into
the location mentally by doing intense research on the
history and reputation of the environment.
I obtain pictures, video, EVP, and accounts of direct
experiences of people who have been there. I immerse
myself in the subject matter. I put myself there in my
mind. At the time that I am projecting my consciousness
into this environment. I am also carrying my arsenal of
personal protection. Because I am not there does not
mean I am immune to the environment.
I am projecting myself. As I mentioned earlier the more
you practice a ritual or imitate an act in this world the
stronger it becomes in the unseen world. I believe that all
or at least most of us have astral forms. Strengthening our
astral bodies is very beneficial overall
The majority of psychic, magical, astral, and supernatural
attacks occur on a psychological battlefront. These attacks
occur as an assault on the mind and senses which lead
to a physical decline. A loss of control and confusion are
what usually leads to the most catastrophic of attacks.
The realities of being crossed, obsessed, and possessed,
are all symptoms and causes of magical, astral, psychic,
psychological, and supernatural attacks.

Of course there is the idea that we are under constant attack and surveillance of various alphabet agencies, superior alien life forms, and some things that we can not even imagine. Even if those things are true it is probably best not to focus too much on those possibilities. That type of obsessive paranoid behavior is what you want to try to avoid altogether. I have done private investigations in peoples homes. I noticed an alarming trend. The people involved started allowing whatever it was that was plaguing them to change their normal routines and behaviors. They seemed to be at their closest points of breaking and complete surrender. The stress of the haunting attack started taking its toll. Hauntings and possessions have exhausted people to death

Depending on the severity of the haunting it was peoples sleep patterns and meal times that changed. People would stop having regular or shared meals. Sometimes they sleep together in one room. They even avoid an area at all costs. Some people never leave the house in the fear that something might happen. At this point the haunting has control and they are in a perilous place. So much mental and emotional stress eventually destroys your physical health.

If any of this is true then it would be best to hold it all at arm's length at times. I have an example of this concerning writing this book. I started this project with the true crime section. If you have read to this part of the book then you have probably read that section. At this point of the book, I have not finished that part yet. I had to step away from that subject matter for a while. In the meantime I have primarily written the rest of the book.

I just had to set it down. I was pouring over the crime scene photos and all of the morbid details involved in these series of events. The details were all quite bizarre indeed. I felt stuck, aggravated, and uninspired. Instead, I felt obsessed. My clarity was lost. Any period of intense study can cause similar effects. Every time I would talk to someone I would inundate them with the grizzly details. Anton Lavey called people who only talk about the occult, occult-niks. Lavey thought that they were boring as hell. Phil Hine defines the obsession as magicitus.

All of these topics or any topic could create an obsession. So it is not just the subject matter but the need and desire that is behind it as well. Just like becoming obsessed with the occult, parapsychology, religion, and even Star Wars. Somehow you just have to set it down. All of these topics are fascinating, life-changing, or at least entertaining. If they were not then there would be no point in writing this book.

Usually it is us who gets ourselves in the most trouble. I feel that we are responsible for most of our suffering. We can choose just to ignore all of the mystery in life and accept everything we see at face value. We can just avoid all of the things that make us uncertain and uncomfortable. Just simply take what other people decide is right for you and how you live your life. Right? Not for me. I guess not for you either. In the last few pages we are going to learn how to increase our power and how to gain a better understanding of it.

How Do You Relate?

What brings you strength? When do you feel powerful and the most capable? What is a symbol you resonate with? Do you have a sense of faith? To build your arsenal you are going to have to have the right tools. You are going to have to create a healthy relationship with the things that you use for protection. Learn not to take your relationship with your religion, craft, handgun, or your spirit guides for granted.

Any system is full of archetypes and symbols. One of my very favorites symbols is the Sacred Chao. Pronounced (sacred cow), I have been drawing this symbol for as long as I could grab a pencil and draw lines and circles. That's it down there in the corner. There is a lot of meaning and information packed into that symbol for me. Find a symbol or create one. Spend time each day looking at it. Illustrate it and add your touches to stylize it.

Concentrate on the symbol. Stare at it for as long as you can. That thing will happen when you eventually close your eyes. You will be able to see the symbol, and it will appear to be kind of floating there. What I want you to do now is try to hold it there in your mind. Learn to keep it in place. It will try to fade away and jitter around but if you keep at it you will eventually be able to hold it in place. Once you can consistently maintain the symbol in place try manipulating and changing it. Modify the color and size of it. Make it spin or fade away and solidify again.

You can refer back to the occult section for a more detailed explanation of object concentration. Developing this ability is not as complicated as it seems. Visualization is something we do naturally. It is possible to do what I am describing. You just have to see the value in practicing this discipline and any other. It takes time and practice but the payoff is fresh.

Sometimes people who have been working in groups share visualizations. This phenomenon is also a mass hallucination but in any case it happens. Rather or not it is a combination of the person who is seeing it, their powers of visualization, or the strength of the individual's ability to project the image. It happens. Not all of the time but I have experienced this my self.

So what do you do with this now that you have spent countless hours staring at esoteric symbols and recalling them clearly in your mind's eye? Use that logo to protect yourself, your environment, and other nouns. That's right! Try projecting that image into your home, car, onto people, and anytime you feel like you are under attack or maybe just need to clear your head and get your barrings. Visualize the symbol covering you. Try to imagine it as a tattoo or get a tattoo of the glyph.

Visualization is useful when it comes to occult practices. For many techniques call for the use of symbols and scenarios. Work on these techniques for a period until you feel capable of executing them. Be honest with yourself in the course of your progress. Keep track of your results and make notes of the experiences. Once you have come to this point keep practicing, but start working on grounding yourself as well.

THE KABBALISTIC CROSS

The ritual that I am about to describe to you is one of my personal favorites. Another reason I am adding this technique is that it is the preliminary process for the lesser banishing ritual of the pentagram. The kabbalistic cross is a way to orient yourself in all places, at all times, and to create a balance in your true will. In this model, the source of all energy and the material world represent 2 spheres Malkuth (the material world) and Kether (the source of all things).

The connection is the link that more or less creates life. Both the seen and the unseen are united. You are fixed firmly between them. A brilliant line of energy runs through you from the top of your head through the bottom of your feet. Kether is a place of higher consciousness. Forming this link connects you to a spiritual realm and the Earth simultaneously. While facing the east stand in a relaxed fashion. Visualize a bright ball of light above your head. Imagine standing on top of the Earth as if you are a colossal being.

Reach up with your hand, wand, or dagger and draw a line of pure bright light that is radiating from that ball above your head down to the planet that you are standing on. Imagine yourself there with the light running through your body from the top of your head through the bottom of your feet and then plunging into the earth below you. There you are joined in a union between the heavens and the Earth. So now that you are there it is time to complete the cross.

The next steps involve creating a balance in your true will. Being is simply being without the spark of doing. Create the line of doing by connecting another 2 spheres called Geburah (judgment) and Chesed (mercy). Visualize a bright red sphere at your right shoulder draw a line of bright light to the second sphere of bright blue light to your left shoulder. Now reverse the route back to the right shoulder from the left shoulder to complete the connection.

The line of doing represents your ability to take action and utilize your true will. The line between mercy and judgment gives us the capacity to make choices, take action, and wield our true will with responsibility and clarity to make the right decisions and to take the proper course of action. Love, hate, mercy, and judgment are all balanced on this line.

A FEW SIMPLE STEPS

In step 1 vibrate the word (Atah) "though art" and touch your forehead while drawing the line of light to your groin.

In step 2 while drawing the line, once you get to your groin vibrate the word (Malkuth) "the kingdom" and tap your groin. Continue drawing the line down your body eventually drawing it into the earth beneath you.

In step 3 tap your right shoulder and vibrate the word (Ve Gevurah) "the power" and draw the line to your left shoulder.

In step 4 touch your left shoulder and vibrate the word (Ve Gedulah) "the glory" and draw the line back to your left shoulder.

In step 5 extend your arms horizontally to your sides making the shape of a T. Raise your arms to clasp your hands together over your head. While leaving your palms touching, bring your arms down in front of you, stopping in the area of your heart and vibrate the word (Amen) "forever."

Though art
The Kingdom
The Power and
The Glory
Forever

The Tree of Life is a beautiful model that is full of secrets and mystery. It is considered a staple concerning western occultism. It is believed to have roots that are far reaching. A study of The Kabbalistic Tree of Life is definitely worth the time. There are quite a few exercises related to this model and if you are creative enough you could make your own.

As I suggested this exercise is a means to orient yourself and get a stable footing. I have found this exercise also helps in more ordinary situations as well. Anytime you need to get centered or find your focus you can use this technique. Do not worry if it is hard to visualize all of the steps of the process. Keep doing it. You will be able to with enough time.

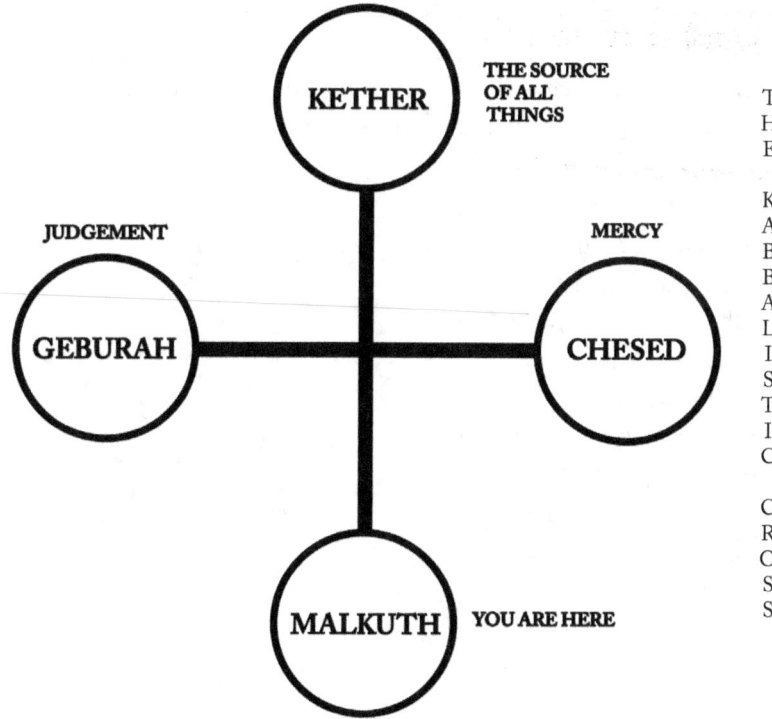

As we move forward it is going to be necessary to take a look at the pentagram. A pentagram is a 5 sided star-shaped polygon. In Greek they are called pentagrammon. Another old reference to the pentagram is the Cuniform logogram for the word corner. The pentagram is another valuable symbol commonly used in occult practices. You have seen it on album covers, books, and all kinds of other places. The pentacle is used for purposes amongst a variety of disciplines and religious concepts.

The pentacles share a similar significance in meaning to all who use it. The pentacle is a model that contains the 4 elements and as a result spirit. The pentacle is magical to me because it is an example of the sum being greater than the whole of the parts. The idea is that all of the elements combined create spirit and the astral residue that manifests as a result of the unseen world. The elements air, earth, fire, and water are what make up our planet and all of the things that are necessary for survival.

Just like the sacred chao. One could project a pentagram in the same fashion. The shape seems to fit over the human form quite nicely. There are many applications for the pentagram. Invoking, evoking, and banishing are other common uses.

Invoking is to call to something. Evoking is to call something out. Banishing is to order something to be gone. You may invoke a being to make itself present. You may evoke a being to conjure or to come forth into space. Think of the word evocative. When something is evocative it brings thoughts and feelings into your mind. Invoking is an invitation as evoking is more of a command to appear or to become present in some form. Banishing is a little more self-explanatory.

In some schools of witchcraft and Wicca entities are evoked into shapes outside of the magic circle. The God and the Goddess if applicable are invoked into the magic circle. For our purposes we are focusing on banishing. Clearing a space has obvious benefits. There are many kinds of banishing techniques which are unique to their related systems and personal preferences of the practitioner. This lesser banishing ritual of the pentagram is very powerful. If practiced on a daily basis the routine can be very beneficial to an environment.

Draw 4 pentagrams that surround you. You will draw 1 pentagram for each direction. Starting in the east and eventually come back to the same point. When using the lesser banishing ritual of the pentagram, you will be drawing the banishing pentagram of the Earth. The pentagram is created by starting at the point of the pentagram that corresponds with the element earth. (See the figure on the previous page) Orient yourself with this illustration. 1. With your right hand draw a line of bright light from your left foot diagonally up to a spot directly above your head. The point of the pentagram that corresponds with spirit.

2. Now draw a line diagonally down from just above your head to the point of the pentagram that corresponds with the element fire at your right foot. 3. Draw a line diagonally up to the point of the pentagram, which corresponds with the element air right above your left shoulder. 4. Next, draw a line straight acros, to the point of the pentagram, which corresponds to the element water, just above your right shoulder. 5. Finally draw the last line diagonally dow, back to the point of the pentagram that corresponds to the element earth.

The result should be a brilliant unicursal pentagram, that is flaming in front of you at arm's length from your body. Once again you may or may not be able to visualize the bright lines that make up the pentagram. Do not fret. Just keep practicing the motions until you can do it comfortably. Try not to worry about the result. Just focus on the doing until the actions are familiar to you. Try performing the actions with your eyes closed. Sometimes that helps with the visualizing.

For each direction perform the same actions while vibrating the corresponding words for each direction listed below. After creating the final pentagram you should be facing the north. After vibrating the last word turn back to the east where you began. Just like the kabbalistic cross for each step of the ritual you vibrate a word that corresponds with your action and the creation of each pentagram.

1. To the east vibrate (YAD-HEH-VAHV-HEH)
2. To the south vibrate (AH-DOH-NYE)
3. To the west vibrate (EH-HEH-YEH)
4. To the north vibrate (AH-GLAH)

What I mean by vibrate is say the word like you are chanting it. Slowly roll out the syllables from the bottom of your diaphragm. Say the words with meaning and purpose. It feels strange that is okay because it is kind of weird. I mean you are about to invoke archangels to stand with you. Do not be surprised if things get a little...You know...Unsettling. Do not get distracted continue with the ritual and keep your composure. By performing this ritual you are in agreement that the impossible could be possible and that the paranormal is either a side effect or a direct product of performing this ritual. The next step involves inviting 4 archangels to stand with you. Each archangel corresponds to a position around your body. When you have returned to the eastern position stand with your arms outstretched to your sides. Make the shape of a T again. Say in a loud and clear voice, "Before me stands Raphael." Vibrate the name Raphael just like you vibrated the words in the last step. Draw the name out. (RAH-FEY-EL)

Now invoke the name of Gabriel. Say in a loud and clear voice, "Behind me stands Gabriel." (GAHB-RAY-EL) Next invoke the name Michael. Speak in a loud clear voice, "On my right-hand stands Michael." (MIH-KIE-EL)
Finally, invoke the name, Uriel. Say in a loud, clear voice. "On my left-hand stands Uriel." (UHR-RIE-EL)

Take a moment consider what you are doing. In a genuine sense you may be surrounded by celestial energy entities. So give that a minute to simmer. Take a little bit of time to do some research on these entities. Get to know them. Find out about their correspondences.

After you have oriented yourself in time and space, you have created a direct link which runs between the seen and unseen world and yourself. You have created balance in your true will by drawing a line that connects you to the concepts of mercy and judgment. Allowing you to act with compassion and reason. You have surrounded yourself in all directions by flaming pentagrams which have been created from the source of all energy. Archangels have been called to join you and you are about to end the ritual. Now say in a loud clear voice, "Around me flames the pentagram, in the center, I am a star. Within me shines the 5 rayed star."

That is the Lesser banishing ritual of the pentagram. The ceremony I have described here is different than the one I perform. Over time and practice you will develop your relationship with this ritual as well. What I have described here is a very bare bones version that is good to use to get into practice. After a period the whole process will not take you very long.

That is it. As I promised I have given you the means to protect yourself and to enhance and understand your sense of power. You must perform these practices. Not doing them will yield no results. Doing them will probably bring some unexpected and potentially exciting results. Remember I would love to hear about your personal experiences. Find the means to contact me in this book. I would love to hear from you.

THE STEPS

Part 1

Step 1. Perform the kabbalistic cross to open the ceremony

Part 2

Step 2. Face the east, draw the banishing pentacle of the earth, point to the center and vibrate the name (Yahweh)

Step 3. Make a connecting line to the south and draw the banishing pentacle of the earth, point the connecting line to the center, and vibrate the name (Adonai)

Step 4. Carry the connecting line to the west, draw the banishing pentacle of the earth, point the connecting line to the center, and vibrate the name (Ehehyeh)

Step 5. Carry the connecting line to the north, draw the banishing pentacle of the earth, point the connecting line to the center, and vibrate the name (Aglah)

Part 3

With your hands out to your sides and your body in the shape of a T, call to the archangels

Step 1. Before me stands (Raphael)
Step 2. Behind me stands (Gabriel)
Step 3. On my right hand (Michael)
Step 4. On my left hand (Uriel)

Part 4

Step 1. In a loud, clear voice say-

Around me flames the pentagram, in the center, I am a star. Within me shines the 5 rayed star.
All around me are stars.

Part 5

Step 1. Perform the kabbalistic cross to close the ceremony

Part 6

Take notes of how you felt the ceremony went. Take some time to get grounded. Pay attention to your environment and the way you feel. Use the chance to take in the experience. How do you feel? How long did it take? Did anything strange happen? Every ritual is an opportunity for experience. I can not stress the importance of documenting your procedures.

AFTERWARDS

It is right about 3:37 am. I am watching John Carpenter's: They Live! One of my faves. **Keith David is taking Roddy Piper to the homeless encampment to get a plate of food and a safe place to sleep.** It is 4/02/2017. I have just finished this book. I started this project on 03/23/2016. It has been a little over a year. I have finally come to the end of this compendium. Writing this book is a great accomplishment for me. Some of the people who helped me write this book probably don't even know that they helped. I have created a proper thank you page to commemorate them.

Now Roddy Piper is in the middle of some raid in the homeless camp by the local authorities. Roddy is doing well to keep his attackers at bay. The topics we have discussed in this book are mainly taboo things. These taboo subjects have gained popularity and acceptance over time. I have always asked myself, what is more bizarre than something that is paranormal? My answer is the SUPERNORMAL! I have always seen the paranormal as the supernormal. Not being aware or fully understanding something does not mean that it is not always present or that it is not having an impact on your life.

Many of us live in a state of denial. I think that it is because of how we perceive ourselves and the world as a whole. People tend to live as an image of how they want people to see them. More often than not what we want to be and what we are is not the same thing. The world is changing. People are more open about what they want and how they want to live. Of course, sometimes this gets pretty annoying when people are shoving their wants and needs down your throat.

I turned 40 this year. Things have changed quite a bit. What is seen as acceptable is very different than the type of expectations that were pushed off on me by society? Professional environments are full of people with tattoos and crazy hair colors. Everybody I know is weird so it is perfect for us. There is that breed of people who will not let go. These people will not budge. They will carry their fear and dogma. That is their choice. **Roddy Piper just found the box of special sunglasses that allows him to see the truth in the world around him: OBEY!**

As fucked up as everything in this world has become I think we are stepping in a right direction. All of the expressive power people have today has been very destructive. I think there may be nothing that is more paranormal than social media. People have relegated long-term friendships to likes and occasional supportive comments. I am pretty sure you know what I mean.

Roddy Piper is about to say that thing about bubble gum before he goes on a beautiful savage killing spree at the bank. We are not at a golden age. I am non-plussed if we are at a pinnacle of humanity. Technology does not make us evolved beings. Look at how we use the tech and how we treat each other. Keep in my mind I am not some tree hugging hippy weirdo. I know it all can't be peace, pot, and microdot but I think we could do a lot better.

This book is the first page of my Necronomicon. I have spent my life building experience as an occultist and a paranormal researcher. A Bizarre Compendium is a small map of the territory. The methods that I have introduced here yield results over time, study, and application. Do it or don't, but just don't half-ass it. **Now that we are at the part where Keith David and Roddy Piper are about to get into that epic brawl in the alley, it is time for me to wrap this up. See you next time!**

SPECIAL THANKS TO A FEW

Over time I have met some genuine individuals.
All of these people helped me in one way or another.

Jenny Hallman (The first person that I always think of)
Eli Cain (For growing into a man that I respect)
Mojo-Walter-Willow-Charmander - Doggerz The Dog (My best animal friends)
Phyllis Freeman & Phillip Cato (You know why)
The Devil (Because it should get its due)
Ganesha (The binder of demons and the destroyer of obstacles)
Scott Medjesky (Too many reasons to state)
Jessie & Sarah Cummings (2 people who know me well)
H.P.. Lovecraft (The strangest person that has ever lived)
Beyond The Darkness (The best paranormal radio show)
Bruce (The Beast) Brayton (one of the few wise people I know)
John Ginder (A pal and a confidant)
Alex Sage (You are just great)
Wanda Kay (For trusting me)
Jeffery Pritchett (My cosmic soul brother)
Drew Bowman (The Destroyer)
Trevor Patton (A genuine individual)
Erin Burr (The Satanic Witch)
WHAM! (A very understanding person)
Tracy Price (My soul sister)
Michelle Castillo (The Gunslinger)
Dana Byard (Because he is a writer)
Harry Bean (For being a Bean & a lot more)
Julie Edwards (A dedicated friend)
Krista Ecret (For being honest)
Dushawn Miller (Who is metal as fuck)
Nikki Shanks (The Dragon Lady)
Summer Nickleson & the good people of Tony Montana's Grill
The Indianapolis Public Library
George Romero
Anton Lavey
Rod Serling

THE AMAZING

TALKING BOARD!

IT IS AS SIMPLE AS---

YES!

NO!

GOODBYE!

GET YOURS TODAY!

CONTACT BAZ BOT ON FACEBOOK,
AND ORDER A BOARD RIGHT NOW, FROM THE BEYOND!

A Bizarre Compendium Vol. 1

IMAGE GALLERY

Bibliography

(2016, August 31). Retrieved from Week In Weird: http://weekinweird.com/2016/08/31/investigating-the-link-between-the-shadow-man-phenomenon-and-the-terrifying-hat-man/

5 Types Of Brain Waves Frequencies: Gamma, Beta, Alpha, Theta, Delta. (n.d.). Retrieved from Mental Health Daily: http://mentalhealthdaily.com/2014/04/15/5-types-of-brain-waves-frequencies-gamma-beta-alpha-theta-delta/

Bergland, C. (2015, April 17). The Atheletes Way. Retrieved from Psychology Today: https://www.psychologytoday.com/blog/the-athletes-way/201504/alpha-brain-waves-boost-creativity-and-reduce-depression

Bugliosi, G. (1974). Helter Skelter The True Story of The Manson Murders. In V. B. Gentry, Helter Skelter and The True Story of The Manson Murders. W.W. Norton & Company.

Cunningham. (2003). In D. M. Cunningham, A Complete Guide To Entity Creation Creating Magickal Entities. Egregore Publishing.

Demonicpedia. (2016). The Top Hat Demon. Retrieved from Demonicpedia: https://www.demonicpedia.com/demonology/top-hat-demon/

Did Manson Borrow Killer Cult's Beliefs. (1970, January 4). Retrieved from Cielodrive.com: http://www.cielodrive.com/archive/did-manson-borrow-british-cults-beliefs/

Fowler, S. L. (2016, December 16). What Are Shadow People. Retrieved from The Shadow People Archives: http://www.shadowpeople.org/

Gorightl, A. (n.d.). The Process Church of The Final Judgement and Charles Manson. Retrieved from Paranoia The Conspiracy Reader: http://www.paranoiamagazine.com/2012/11/the-process-church-of-the-final-judgment-and-the-manson-family/

Hine. (1995). In P. Hine, Condensed Chaos An Introduction To Chaos Magic. New Falcon Publications.

Kind, F. (2017, Juky 24). The Mantids. Retrieved from Fourth Kind: http://fourthkind.com/the-mantids/

Kraig. (2011). In D. M. Kraig, Modern Magick Twelve Lessons In The High Magickal Arts. Llewellyn.

Lavey. (1969). In A. S. Lavey, The Satanic Bible. Avon.

Pappas, S. (2012, 17 2012). Brain Chemicals That Casue Sleep Paralysis Discovered. Retrieved from Live Science: https://www.livescience.com/21653-brain-chemicals-sleep-paralysis.html

Redfern, N. (2014, December 12). Beware of The Hatman. Retrieved from Mysterious Universe: http://mysteriousuniverse.org/2014/12/beware-of-the-hat-man/

Sanders. (2002). In E. Sanders, The Family. Thunder Mouth Press.

Schlangekraft. (1977). In Schlangekraft, Necronomicon. Avon.

Scientologist Denies Murder Link. (1969, December 13). Retrieved from Cielodrive.com: http://www.cielodrive.com/archive/scientologists-deny-murder-link/

Simon. (2006). In Simon, Dead Names The Dark History of The Necronomicon. Avon.

Symphonicminds. (2007). What Are Brainwaves. Retrieved from Brainworks Train Your Mind: http://www.brainworksneurotherapy.com/what-are-brainwaves

Tegtmeier. (1990). In R. Tegtmeier, Practical Sigil Magic Creating Personal Symbols for. Llewellyn Publications.

Terry. (1987). In M. Terry, The Ultimate Evil The truth About The Cult Murders Son of Sam and Beyond. Barnes & Nobles.

Waggoner, B. M. (1998, 12 29). The Edicaran Period. Retrieved from The University of California Museum of Palentolgy: http://www.ucmp.berkeley.edu/vendian/ediacaran.php

Whitcomb. (1993). In B. Whitcomb, The Magicians Companion A Practical & Encyclopedic Guide to Magical Religious Symbolism. Llewellyn.

Whitney, B. (2015, July 20). The Process Church of The Final Judgement Lives On. Retrieved from Disnfo: http://disinfo.com/2015/07/process-church-final-judgment-lives/

A Bizarre Compendium Vol. 1

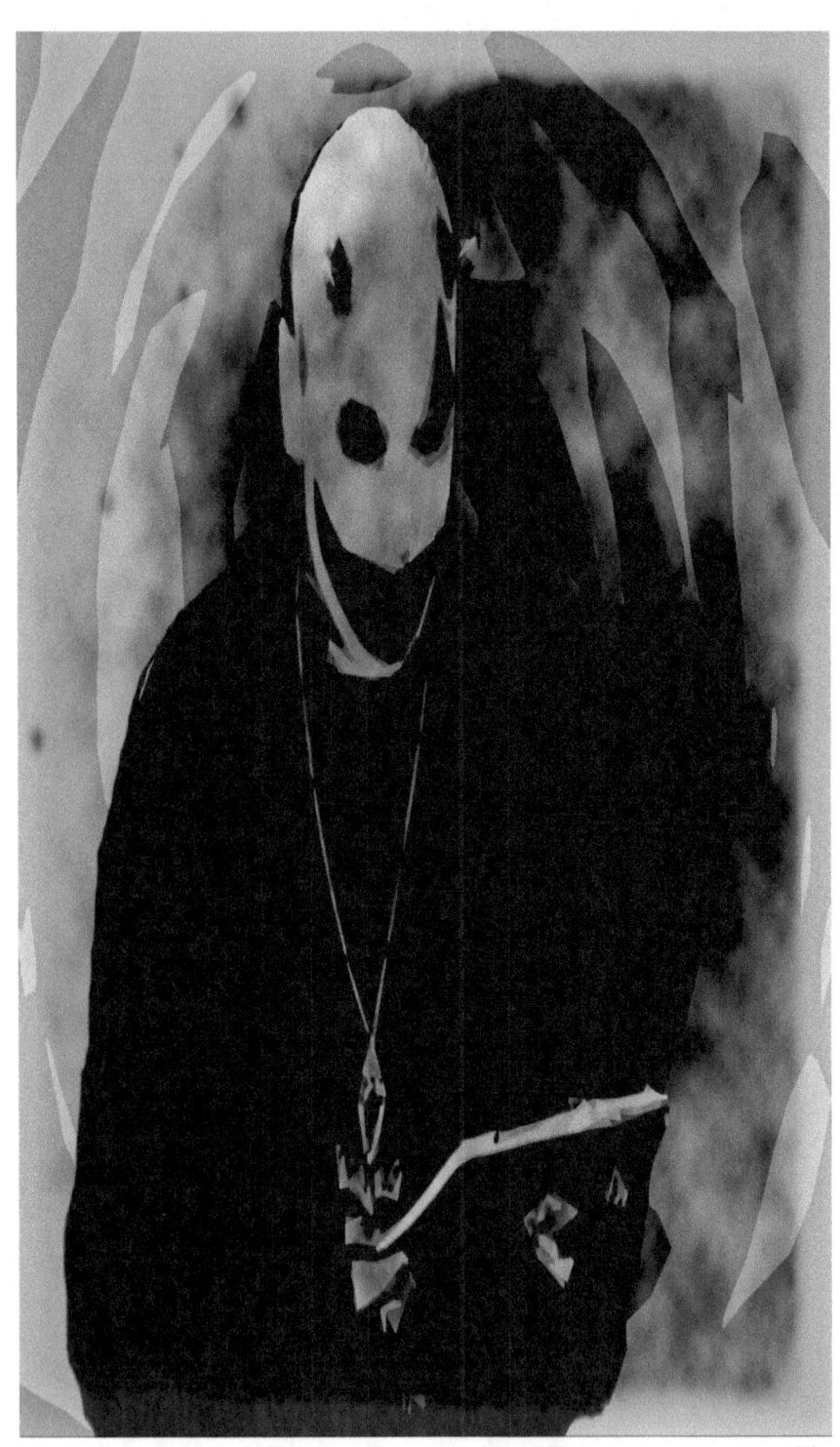

A Bizarre Compendium Vol. 1

www.ingramcontent.com/pod-product-compliance
Lightning Source LLC
Chambersburg PA
CBHW070107290526
45789CB00005B/1952